"John Beck has produced a masterful guide to the lands of the Bible."

Paul H. Wright, president, Jerusalem University College, Israel

"Travelers to Israel often ask me if there is a guidebook I recommend. John Beck has provided me with a definitive answer: *The Holy Land for Christian Travelers*. I won't travel to Israel again without this book."

J. Carl Laney, professor of biblical literature, Western Seminary, Portland, Oregon

"The maps, artistic reconstructions, site explanations, timelines, etc., help make this guide the best one on the market. You won't want to travel to Israel without this guide in your backpack."

Michael A. Grisanti, professor of Old Testament and director of TMS Israel Studies program, The Master's Seminary

"No tourist ought to land in Israel without this valuable guide. Over time, this guide will become your dog-eared, marked-up, and duct-taped traveling partner."

Jim Halbert, lead pastor, Crossroads Community Church, Nampa, Idaho

"This book provides an outstanding introduction to the land of Israel, as well as accurate descriptions of the most important sites."

Todd Bolen, professor of biblical studies, The Master's University; photographer, BiblePlaces.com

"This book offers essential orientation for understanding just how the land and geography are a vital part of the biblical story."

C. Chappell Temple, lead pastor, Christ Church (UMC), Sugar Land, Texas

"I now look at the land and read the Word of God with a new pair of eyes."

Robert Chew, senior pastor, Moriah Bible Presbyterian Church, Singapore

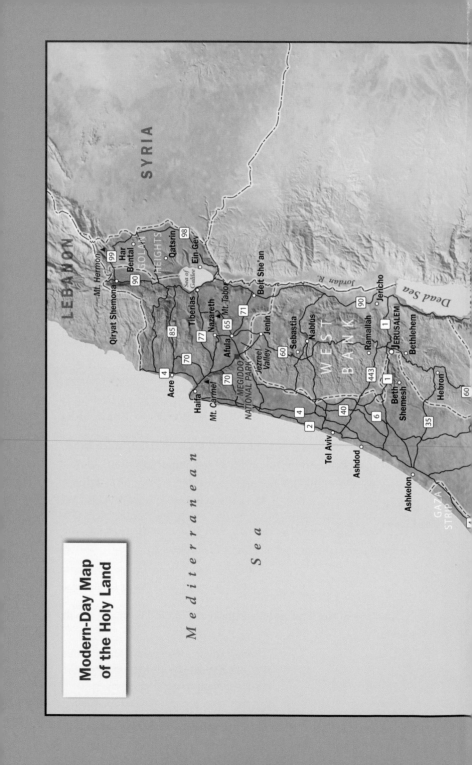

Modern-Day Map of the Holy Land

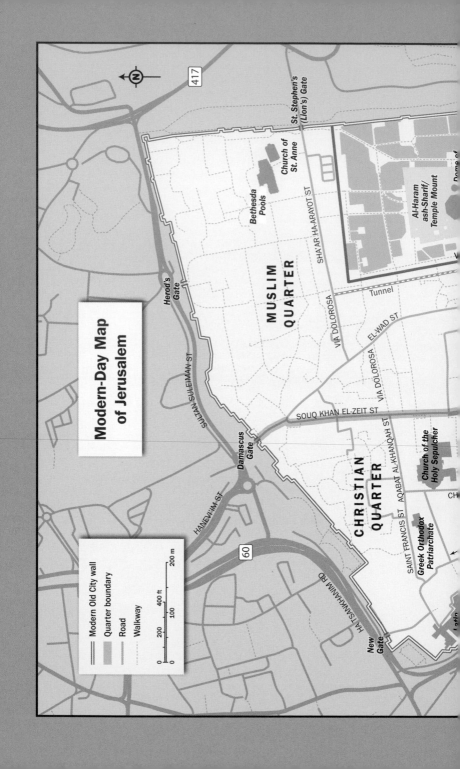

Modern-Day Map
of Jerusalem

Legend:
Modern Old City wall
Quarter boundary
Road
Walkway

0   200   400 ft
0   100   200 m

417

Herod's Gate

St. Stephen's (Lion's) Gate

Church of St. Anne

Bethesda Pools

SULTAN SULEIMAN ST

SHA'AR HA-ARAYOT ST

Al-Haram ash-Sharif / Temple Mount

Dome of

MUSLIM QUARTER

VIA DOLOROSA

Tunnel

EL-WAD ST

Damascus Gate

HANEVI'IM ST

SOUQ KHAN EL-ZEIT ST

VIA DOLOROSA

60

AQABAT AL-KHANQAH ST

SAINT FRANCIS ST

CHRISTIAN QUARTER

Church of the Holy Sepulcher

Greek Orthodox Patriarchate

HATSANKHANIM RD

New Gate

Latin

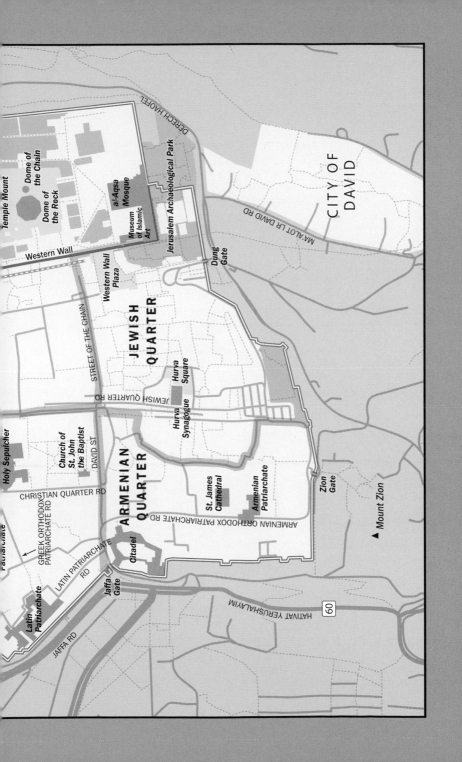

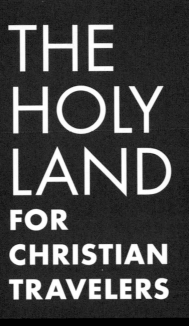

THE HOLY LAND

FOR CHRISTIAN TRAVELERS

An Illustrated Guide to Israel

JOHN A. BECK

BakerBooks

a division of Baker Publishing Group
Grand Rapids, Michigan

Published by Baker Books
a division of Baker Publishing Group
P.O. Box 6287, Grand Rapids, MI 49516-6287
www.bakerbooks.com

Printed in the United States of America

Library of Congress Cataloging-in-Publication Data
Names: Beck, John A., 1956– author.
Title: The Holy Land for Christian travelers : an illustrated guide to Israel / John A. Beck.
Description: Grand Rapids : Baker Books, 2017. | Includes index.
Identifiers: LCCN 2016057225 | ISBN 9780801018923 (pbk.)
Subjects: LCSH: Bible—Geography. | Israel—Description and travel.
Classification: LCC BS630 .B369 2017 | DDC 263/.0425694—dc23
LC record available at https://lccn.loc.gov/2016057225

Interior design by William Overbeeke

18   19   20   21   22   23   7   6   5   4   3   2

■ ■ ■

For Marmy,
my bride,
my soul mate,
and coadventurer,
whose longtime support
for my wanderings
made this publication possible

■ ■ ■

CONTENTS

Look for These Symbols

⭐ Must-see location

📍 Location description

💳 Fees charged

🚫 No payment required

👕 Modest dress required

INTRODUCTION

"The LORD had said to Abram, 'Go from your country, your people and your father's household to the land I will show you.'"

GENESIS 12:1

t is time to go. The Lord is calling you to step away from all that is familiar, just as he once called Abram. He is inviting you to leave your home, your family, and the normal rhythms of life in order to show you a new land. But this is no ordinary place. The promised land shaped Bible events, molded the thinking of men and women of the Bible, and provided the images that communicate the thoughts of God. As you explore this land, you will quickly see that the Bible is at home here. And you will become more at home in your Bible as you travel the promised land.

I know that will happen because it happened to me and because I have seen it happen to others. I have studied the relationship between this Holy Land and the Bible for twenty years. Those years have changed me. During that time I have led more than one thousand people on educational journeys here. Each person has been changed by the experience. So be ready to be transformed. The Lord brings people to the promised land to change them. Expect it. Expect to be changed in ways you cannot yet begin to imagine.

I wrote this guide to help with that change and to achieve the Lord's intentions for your trip to the promised land. Abram made a permanent home here. That is not true for you, so I wrote this guide to help you plan and execute a trip that makes the best use of your limited time. If you are on a guided tour, this guide will help you to find the things most important to the Christian faith and your Bible reading. If you are traveling on your own, this guide will help you to compose an efficient, enjoyable, faith-bolstering journey. Like all international travel, a trip to Israel comes with inherent risks. You should plan a trip that takes into consideration your own physical limitations and the conditions in the state of Israel at the time of your trip. This includes consulting the travel alerts and warnings issued by your home country with regard to travel in the Middle East.

To navigate this land you will first need to navigate the pages of this guide, so let me offer you a few thoughts on its composition. First a word on my selection of sites for inclusion in the book. I started with sites that tour groups are most likely to visit and then added sites critical to our understanding of key Bible stories and Bible passages. As a further aid, I have marked the must-see locations with ★ .

I gathered these important stops into chapters that connect those sites regionally. That is the way you are most likely to encounter them when traveling. For example, I have gathered all the sites in the Jerusalem area or the coastal plain. If you are having trouble finding a specific place you plan to visit, the index of locations will quickly get you to the correct page.

You will find considerable variation in the length of the entries. I determined the length of each entry on the basis of the likelihood of your visiting the site, its contribution to Bible reading, and the degree to which the interpretation of the site is advanced by on-site signs and literature. This allowed me to give you more where there is less otherwise available to you.

Finally, you can expect to find the same kind of content in each site-specific entry. The first paragraph will give you an overview of what the site has to offer. The paragraphs that follow will provide information about the history associated with the site and will guide you around the site to the most important things to see, explaining them as necessary. But most important, this guide will build the vital link between the location, what you are seeing, and your Bible reading. That is where it stands apart from those that focus more on restaurants, hotels, and beaches. It is designed to stimulate insight and reflection in Bible readers who have come to the Holy Land. At the close of each entry, you will find a few pieces of practical information like the site's location (📍), fees (💰 or 🚫), and dress requirements if they apply (👕).

Now it's time to get under way. I am excited to be part of this spiritual journey with you and anxious to see what the Lord is about to do in your life. The horizon of change lies just ahead. May this guide be a blessing to you as you begin this spiritual adventure.

A BRIEF HISTORY
of the LAND

3300–1200 BC: Canaanite Period

3300–2300: Early Bronze Age I–III

Bronze became the primary metal for making tools and weapons as writing developed in the Fertile Crescent. Fortified cities complete with temples and palaces developed in Canaan by about 3000 BC. Abraham's forebears lived in Mesopotamia.

2300–2000: Early Bronze Age IV (Middle Bronze Age)

The larger urban centers collapsed and were replaced by unfortified settlements and camps used by those migrating in rhythm to their animals' needs. Abraham's family arrived in Canaan.

2000–1550: Middle Bronze Age

Larger walled cities and greater signs of wealth returned to Canaan together with a nomadic people known as the Amorites. Abraham's family lived in Canaan until famine drove them to Egypt.

1550–1200: Late Bronze Age

Egypt's power extended over the Canaanite city-states. Moses led the Israelites out of Egypt to Mount Sinai and then to the edge of the promised land. Joshua led Israel in the conquest of Canaan. The time of the judges began.

1200–586 BC: Israelite Period

1200–925: Iron Age I

The Philistines arrived in Canaan and dominated the lowlands using iron technology and chariots. The time of the judges continued and concluded. Philistine dominance propelled the Israelite tribes to seek unification under a king. Samuel anointed Saul and David, Israel's first two kings. Its third king, Solomon, was the last to rule Israel as a united kingdom. By 930 BC the united kingdom became the divided kingdom.

925–586: Iron Age II

Israel was ruled as two kingdoms, each with its own capital and king, yet with a shared spiritual responsibility. As both kingdoms struggled spiritually, the corrective words of prophets like Elijah and Elisha failed to elicit the urgent changes needed in the northern kingdom (Israel). The Lord used the Assyrian Empire to punish Israel. Samaria, the capital of the northern kingdom, was destroyed in 722 BC; its people were removed from their land and scattered around the Assyrian Empire. The southern kingdom (Judah) also failed to make needed changes when chastised by the prophets but survived the Assyrian assault. It succumbed to the Babylonian Empire, which began a series of deportations that took Judeans from the promised land to Babylon (605 BC). The siege and destruction of Jerusalem and its temple followed in 586 BC.

586–539 BC: Neo-Babylonian Period

Daniel and Ezekiel spoke to God's people exiled to Babylon while a small remnant of Jews remained in the land; all awaited an Israelite return to the promised land that was to occur seventy years after their exile began.

538–332 BC: Persian Period

Persia displaced Babylon as the empire that controlled the known world. A Jewish woman by the name of Esther became queen of Persia, and Judah was known as the province of Yehud. Zerubbabel, Ezra, and Nehemiah worked to rebuild the temple in Jerusalem, the walls of Jerusalem, and the faithfulness of the returning exiles sent back to their homeland by Cyrus, the Persian king.

332–167 BC: Early Hellenistic Period

Alexander the Great displaced Persia and established an empire that stretched from Macedonia to India. In the wake of his conquest, Greek became the language of international commerce, and Greek culture flowed throughout the known world. Upon his death in 323 BC, Alexander's generals and their families took the reins of power; the Ptolemies (Greek kings in Egypt) and Seleucids (Greek kings in Syria) battled one another for the upper hand, while the Jews and their land were repeatedly caught in the middle of this fight. The darkest days were associated with the reign of Antiochus IV Epiphanes, whose plan of radical Hellenization sought to eradicate the worship practices that made the Jewish people unique.

167–31 BC: Late Hellenistic Period (Hasmonean)

Jewish revolutionaries led by the Maccabee family fought back against the radical Hellenization of Antiochus IV, reestablished Jewish political autonomy, cleansed the temple, and liberated the Jews so that they could practice their religion without penalty. Jewish kings (Hasmoneans) again ruled Israel and expanded the state's land holdings. The destruction of the Samaritan temple on Mount Gerizim created enmity between Jews and Samaritans that lingered into the time of Jesus. But Hasmonean succession problems brought Rome's unwelcomed presence and the loss of Jewish autonomy by 63 BC. Ptolemaic Egypt maintained its autonomy until it was defeated by Rome in the Battle of Actium (31 BC).

31 BC–AD 324: Roman Period

The Roman senate had appointed Herod the Great as king of Judea in 40 BC. This began his storied political and building career that overlapped with the birth of Jesus. Upon Herod's death, his kingdom was divided among his three sons: Herod Antipas (Galilee and Perea), Herod Philip (Iturea, Traconitis, and Gaulanitis), and Archelaus (Judah). Archelaus was removed from office, and Judea was ruled directly by Roman governors starting in AD 6. The early part of this era was the time of Jesus's ministry on earth, the expansion of the Christian church recorded in the book of Acts, and the letters of the New Testament. The Jewish people revolted twice against Rome. The First Jewish Revolt (AD 66–73) ended with the destruction of the temple in Jerusalem by Titus (AD 70) and the fall of Masada (AD 73). The Second Jewish Revolt (AD 132–35) resulted in widespread destruction and renaming. Jerusalem was now called *Aelia Capitolina* and Judea was renamed *Palestina*. The Jewish oral law known as the Mishnah was put into writing in about AD 200.

AD 324–640: Byzantine Period

With the conversion of the Roman emperor Constantine (AD 306–37), Christianity enjoyed a season of growth under the toleration championed by the Edict of Milan (AD 313). Constantine's mother, Helena, began a vigorous campaign of building churches on locations in Israel associated with the life of Jesus. As pilgrims flocked to this land, some elected to remain and establish monastic communities. There was frequent destruction and rebuilding of Christian compounds during this era, much of it related to the Samaritan uprising (AD 529) and the Persian invasion (AD 614).

AD 640–1099: Early Arab (Islamic) Period

Byzantine rule, weakened by Persian invasion, collapsed quickly in the face of Arabian invaders who captured the city of Jerusalem in AD 638. Respectful of both Judaism and Christianity, these Muslim rulers protected and enhanced Jerusalem with new architecture that celebrated the city's relationship to Islam. The Dome of the Rock was built in AD 691, and the El-Aqsa Mosque in AD 715. The exception to tolerance is linked to the rule of Caliph Hakim, who unleashed a persecution against Christians and their churches. During his rule, the tomb of Jesus at the Church of the Holy Sepulchre was destroyed (AD 1009).

AD 1099–1291: Crusader Period

At the close of the early Arab period, Christians faced increasing restrictions as they sought to visit their holy sites. This led Pope Urban II to call for military action designed to remove those restrictions. During the course of five Crusades, access was restored for European pilgrims, churches were rebuilt or founded, hospitals were established, and castles found their place on this land. Unfortunately the Crusaders also attacked and killed many Muslim and Jewish citizens of this land, imposing a negative image on the Crusades that lives to this day in the memory of many. By the close of the thirteenth century, the Crusaders had been defeated and driven from the promised land, largely because of the efforts of Saladin, the first sultan of Egypt and Syria.

AD 1250–1517: Mameluke Period

In the middle part of the thirteenth century, a class of slave soldiers known as Mamelukes (Arabic for "slaves") rose to power in Egypt and Syria. Given challenges faced on other fronts, they gave little attention to the area of Palestine other than to destroy all the fortifications that might prove useful to those who wished to reoccupy this land. Palestine became a remote outpost.

AD 1517–1918: Ottoman Period

Early in the sixteenth century, the Ottoman Turks dominated the region. At this time Suleiman the Magnificent (1520–66) established the system of walls and gates in Jerusalem known today as the modern Old City wall. In the latter part of this era, increasing geographical and archaeological inquiry brought new understanding of Bible history and culture. During World War I the Ottomans allied themselves with Germany. When the war was lost, Britain became the ruling authority in Palestine.

AD 1918–Present: Modern Period

Between 1920 and 1948 Britain's ability and passion to manage this land as a mandate waned. At the same time, the desire to establish a modern Jewish state was on the rise. In 1947 the United Nations Partition Plan called for the formation of a joint Jewish-Arab state. This state formed in 1948, but with territorial concessions that would come back to haunt this land's history. The modern state of Israel consisted of the territory of the coastal plain and west Jerusalem. The Old City of Jerusalem and the west bank of the Jordan River, including most of the mountainous interior from the Sea of Galilee to the Dead Sea, was given to the modern state of Jordan. The newly formed state of Israel was immediately beset by attacks from without and within, leading to the Israeli War of Independence (or Arab-Israeli War). At the close of this war, the independent Jewish state was confirmed, but it continued to face unrest in the years that followed. The Six-Day War of 1967 dramatically changed the map again. During this war, Israel seized the Old City of Jerusalem and much of the modern Sinai and militarily occupied the Golan Heights and the West Bank.

The GEOGRAPHY
and CLIMATE
of the PROMISED LAND

Geographical Zones

GEOGRAPHICAL ZONE	GEOGRAPHY	CULTURE
Coastal Plain	Low in elevation Generally level terrain close to the Mediterranean Sea	Grain agriculture Easily traveled (International Highway) Easily invaded
Central Mountains	High in elevation Steep-sided mountains and narrow, V-shaped valleys (most prominent in south)	Terraced agriculture for olives and fruit Difficult to travel Difficult to invade
Jordan Rift Valley	Elevations below sea level Sea of Galilee, Jordan River, and Dead Sea	North: fishing and agriculture South: mining for salt and bitumen Lightly traveled because of swamps, large-predator attacks, and high temperatures
Transjordan Plateau	Highest in elevation Mountains and high plateaus	North: grain agriculture and cattle Middle: olives and fruit, sheep and goats South: camels and trade Travel on the King's Highway

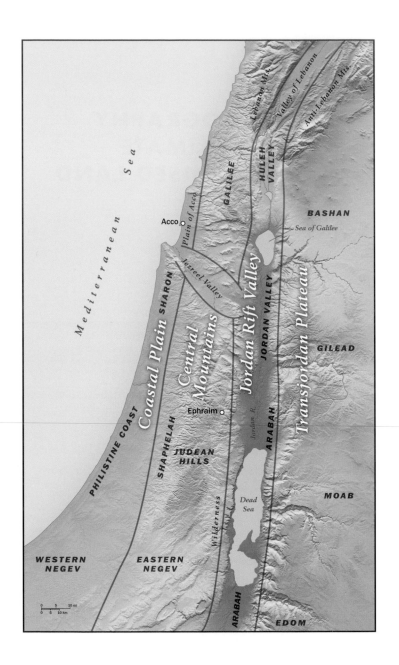

Mediterranean Sea

Lebanon Mts.

Valley of Lebanon

Anti-Lebanon Mts.

GALILEE

HULEH VALLEY

BASHAN

Sea of Galilee

Acco

Plain of Acco

Jezreel Valley

Jordan Rift Valley

JORDAN VALLEY

Coastal Plain

SHARON

Central Mountains

Transjordan Plateau

GILEAD

PHILISTINE COAST

SHAPHELAH

Ephraim

Jordan R.

ARABAH

JUDEAN HILLS

Wilderness

Dead Sea

MOAB

WESTERN NEGEV

EASTERN NEGEV

ARABAH

EDOM

0   5   10 mi
0 5 10 km

The Agricultural Year

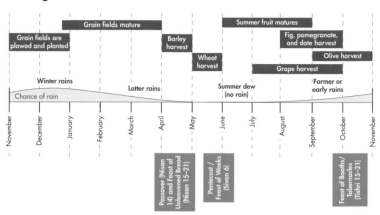

Seasons and Culture

SEASON	MONTHS	CLIMATE	CULTURE IN BIBLE TIMES
Summer	May–September	Stable atmosphere	Overland travel
		Sunny skies	Mediterranean shipping
		Warmer temperatures (Jerusalem average high, 83°F)	Season for war
			Maturing of olives, dates, grapes, and figs
		Pleasant westerly sea breeze	People look for ways to stay cool
		No rain	Cisterns empty and water table drops
		High humidity and dewfall	Flowers wither
			Pastures dry out
Winter	October–April	Unstable atmosphere	Overland travel diminishes
		Frequent cloudy days	Mediterranean shipping ceases
		Cooler temperatures (Jerusalem average high, 63°F)	Season of peace
			Maturing and harvesting grain
		Gusty winds	People look for ways to warm up
		Rain and occasional snow	Cisterns fill and water table recharges
			Flowers spring to life
			Pastures turn green

Winds

WIND	SOURCE	CULTURAL IMPACT	EXAMPLES
Pressure-Induced Winds	Created as air moves between high and low pressure areas	High winds associated with deep lows of the winter season that can destroy structures and threaten shipping on the Mediterranean Sea	Ezekiel 13:13–14; 27:26; Matthew 7:27; Acts 27:13–14
Mediterranean Sea Breeze	Created during the summer months when air cooled over the Mediterranean Sea moves inland to replace the warm air rising over the land	Celebrated winds that provide natural air-conditioning and a predictable breeze that farmers used to winnow their grain	Job 21:18; Psalm 1:4; Isaiah 17:13
Sharqiya	Created when cool air on the ridges above the Sea of Galilee descends violently into the lake basin	Destructive and unpredictable winds that can catch even experienced fishermen off guard and fill them with terror	Matthew 14:22–24; Mark 4:35–37; Luke 8:22–25
Khamsin	Dry south and southeast winds that bring high temperatures and fill the air with gritty, yellow clouds of dust as the atmosphere changes between seasons	Harsh winds that suddenly and totally decimate pastures and wildflowers in early summer and that irritate people and shorten tempers; a symbol of divine judgment	Psalm 103:15–16; Isaiah 27:8; Jeremiah 18:17; Hosea 12:1; Luke 12:55

Water

In contrast to Egypt or Mesopotamia, where major rivers and irrigation provide access to fresh water, the promised land is dependent on rainfall (Deut. 11:10–11). Because rainfall virtually ceases for seven months of the year (April–October), the rainwater has to be captured or underground water has to be accessed to assure a yearlong supply.

SOURCE FOR WATER	CHARACTERISTICS
Spring	Springs occur naturally when the land's surface coincides with the elevation of the water table.
	They offer clean, filtered water with minimum need for development or maintenance.
Well	Wells are shafts dug down to the water table.
	Their sides are lined with fieldstones to prevent collapse.
	A cap and cover are added to prevent evaporation and contamination.
	Yearly maintenance is required.
Cistern	Cisterns are underground chambers dug into bedrock to store runoff water captured during the rainy season.
	They have a narrow neck near the surface, which widens into a bell-shaped body.
	A cap and cover are added to prevent evaporation and contamination.
	Yearly maintenance is required to replace the plaster that waterproofs the sides.
Aqueduct, Tunnel, and Reservoir	These major construction projects, undertaken by strong central governments, are meant to access, move, and store water at locations more convenient for those living in large cities.
	Yearly maintenance is required.

Rainfall

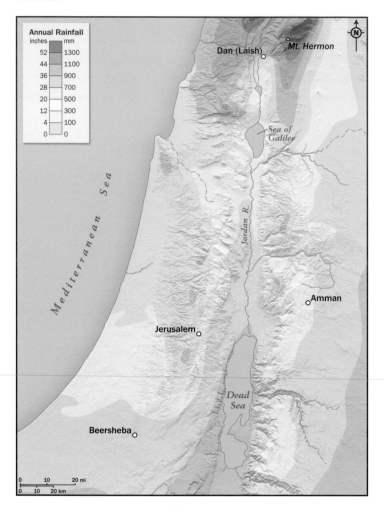

Annual Rainfall

inches	mm
52	1300
44	1100
36	900
28	700
20	500
12	300
4	100
0	0

Dan (Laish)

Mt. Hermon

Sea of Galilee

Mediterranean Sea

Jordan R.

Amman

Jerusalem

Dead Sea

Beersheba

0   10   20 mi
0   10   20 km

ITINERARIES

If you are composing your own itinerary for one or more days of your experience in the Holy Land, this section offers suggested stops for trips of varying length. The order in which the sites are listed reflects just one possible itinerary. Your personal plan will depend on a number of factors including where you are spending the night, the length of your touring day, the particular day you will be visiting these locations, the amount of time you wish to spend at each location, and your level of interest in a particular site. As you make your plan, be sure to take into account driving or walking time between sites as well as the opening and closing times at the sites you plan to visit on the day you plan to visit.

Three Days in Jerusalem

⟳ DAY ONE | Old City of Jerusalem Area

- ‣ Church of the Holy Sepulchre (Church of the Resurrection)
- ‣ Garden Tomb (Gordon's Calvary)

- ‣ Bethesda Pools (Saint Anne's Church)
- ‣ Ecce Homo Convent of the Sisters of Zion
- ‣ Chapels of Flagellation and Condemnation
- ‣ Burnt House
- ‣ Wohl Archaeological Museum
- ‣ Upper Room
- ‣ Saint Peter Gallicantu

⮕ DAY TWO | Old City of Jerusalem Area

- ‣ Temple Mount (Haram esh-Sharif)
- ‣ Jerusalem Archaeological Park
- ‣ Western Wall (*HaKotel*)
- ‣ Broad Wall
- ‣ City of David
- ‣ Akeldama and Hinnom Valley
- ‣ Via Dolorosa
- ‣ Tower of David Museum (Citadel)

⮕ DAY THREE | Jerusalem outside the Old City

- ‣ Kidron Valley Overlook
- ‣ Mount Scopus Observation Point and First-Century Tomb
- ‣ Chapel of the Ascension (Mosque of the Ascension)
- ‣ Pater Noster Church (Eleona Church)
- ‣ Dominus Flevit
- ‣ Church of All Nations (Basilica of Agony)
- ‣ Tisch Family Zoological Gardens
- ‣ Israel Museum

Five Days in Jerusalem and Judea

DAY ONE | Old City of Jerusalem Area

- Church of the Holy Sepulchre (Church of the Resurrection)
- Garden Tomb (Gordon's Calvary)
- Bethesda Pools (Saint Anne's Church)
- Ecce Homo Convent of the Sisters of Zion
- Chapels of Flagellation and Condemnation
- Burnt House
- Wohl Archaeological Museum
- Upper Room
- Saint Peter Gallicantu

DAY TWO | Old City of Jerusalem Area

- Temple Mount (Haram esh-Sharif)
- Jerusalem Archaeological Park
- Western Wall (*HaKotel*)
- Broad Wall
- City of David
- Akeldama and Hinnom Valley
- Via Dolorosa
- Tower of David Museum (Citadel)
- Israel Museum

DAY THREE | Mount of Olives and Bethlehem

- Kidron Valley Overlook
- Mount Scopus Observation Point and First-Century Tomb
- Chapel of the Ascension (Mosque of the Ascension)

- Pater Noster Church (Eleona Church)
- Dominus Flevit
- Church of All Nations (Basilica of Agony)
- Bethlehem and Shepherds' Fields
- Herodium (Herodion) National Park

DAY FOUR | Dead Sea and Judean Wilderness

- Masada National Park
- En Gedi Nature Reserve
- Qumran National Park
- Dead Sea
- Jericho of the New Testament (Tulul Abu El-Alaiq)
- Jericho of the Old Testament (Tell es-Sultan)
- Judean Wilderness (from Wadi Qelt)

DAY FIVE | Judean Hill Country and the Shephelah

- Ein Kerem
- Neot Kedumim Park
- Beth Shemesh
- Elah Valley (from Tel Azekah)
- Beit Guvrin National Park
- Lachish
- Hebron (Al-Khalil)
- Gezer

Twelve Days throughout Israel

⟲ DAY ONE | Jerusalem

- ▸ Church of the Holy Sepulchre (Church of the Resurrection)
- ▸ Garden Tomb (Gordon's Calvary)
- ▸ Bethesda Pools (Saint Anne's Church)
- ▸ Ecce Homo Convent of the Sisters of Zion
- ▸ Chapels of Flagellation and Condemnation
- ▸ Burnt House
- ▸ Wohl Archaeological Museum
- ▸ Upper Room
- ▸ Saint Peter Gallicantu

⟲ DAY TWO | Jerusalem

- ▸ Temple Mount (Haram esh-Sharif)
- ▸ Jerusalem Archaeological Park
- ▸ Western Wall (*HaKotel*)
- ▸ Broad Wall
- ▸ City of David
- ▸ Akeldama and Hinnom Valley
- ▸ Via Dolorosa
- ▸ Tower of David Museum (Citadel)
- ▸ Israel Museum

⟲ DAY THREE | Mount of Olives and Bethlehem

- ▸ Kidron Valley Overlook
- ▸ Mount Scopus Observation Point and First-Century Tomb
- ▸ Chapel of the Ascension (Mosque of the Ascension)

- ▸ Pater Noster Church (Eleona Church)
- ▸ Dominus Flevit
- ▸ Church of All Nations (Basilica of Agony)
- ▸ Bethlehem and Shepherds' Fields
- ▸ Herodium (Herodion) National Park

⟳ DAY FOUR | Dead Sea and Judean Wilderness

- ▸ Masada National Park
- ▸ En Gedi Nature Reserve
- ▸ Qumran National Park
- ▸ Dead Sea
- ▸ Jericho of the New Testament (Tulul Abu El-Alaiq)
- ▸ Jericho of the Old Testament (Tell es-Sultan)
- ▸ Judean Wilderness (from Wadi Qelt)

⟳ DAY FIVE | Benjamin and Samaria

- ▸ Nebi Samuel National Park
- ▸ Shiloh
- ▸ Jacob's Well
- ▸ Shechem (Tell Balata)
- ▸ Samaria/Sebaste

⟳ DAY SIX | Judean Hill Country and the Shephelah

- ▸ Ein Kerem
- ▸ Neot Kedumim Park
- ▸ Gezer
- ▸ Beth Shemesh
- ▸ Elah Valley (from Tel Azekah)

- ▸ Beit Guvrin National Park
- ▸ Hebron (Al-Khalil)
- ▸ Lachish

⟳ DAY SEVEN | Negev

- ▸ Beersheba
- ▸ Arad
- ▸ En Avdat National Park
- ▸ Makhtesh Ramon
- ▸ Timna Valley National Park

⟳ DAY EIGHT | Coastal Plain

- ▸ Ashkelon
- ▸ Jaffa (ancient Joppa)
- ▸ Caesarea Maritima

⟳ DAY NINE | Jezreel Valley

- ▸ Mukhraqa Monastery on Mount Carmel
- ▸ Haifa and Israel's Ancient Maritime Culture
- ▸ Megiddo
- ▸ Mount Tabor

⟳ DAY TEN | Golan Heights

- ▸ Hazor
- ▸ Dan
- ▸ Banias (Paneas, Caesarea Philippi)
- ▸ Har Bental (Mount Bental)
- ▸ Katzrin Historic Village

- Gamla Nature Reserve
- Bethsaida (Julias)

DAY ELEVEN | Sea of Galilee

- Sea of Galilee
- Korazim National Park (Chorazin)
- Capernaum
- Heptapegon (Tabgha)
- Mount of the Beatitudes
- Mount Arbel National Park and Nature Reserve
- Kursi National Park

DAY TWELVE | Lower Galilee and the Harod Valley

- Nazareth
- Mount Precipice (Nazareth)
- Sepphoris (Zippori National Park)
- Jezreel
- En Harod
- Beth Shean National Park

THINGS TRAVELERS
NEED to KNOW

Your trip to Israel will focus on the past, but a number of present realities will affect your time here. I offer the following information to help you have a safer and more efficient trip through the promised land.

1. *Identification.* The modern state of Israel requires everyone to carry personal identification. At any point in the trip, you may be asked to produce your passport. Make it a practice to carry it with you whenever you are touring.

2. *Modest Dress.* Clothing standards will apply at many sites mentioned in this guide. In some cases this calls for modest dress (indicated by 🔘), which means that both men and women need to wear garments that cover both the knees and shoulders. Men must remove their caps or hats in certain cases and wear them in others. If you enter an area where you are uncertain about appropriate dress, watch for signs and take note of how the local residents dress.

3. *Respectful Photographing of People.* Local residents do not view themselves as part of the touring experience. They may or may not permit you to take their photograph. It is always best to ask. And if they agree, they may expect you to pay them for taking their photograph.

4. *Respectful Treatment of Antiquity Sites.* Part of your learning experience will involve interaction with the archaeological remains found in Israel's national parks. Realize that these treasures of the past can be harmed by mistreatment; please be respectful of them. Furthermore, the local residents do not view these ruins as playgrounds and will be offended if we treat their cultural artifacts with a lack of respect. You will gain their respect when you show respect for the artifacts that are part of their heritage.

5. *Respectful Treatment of the Natural World.* This guide will also encourage you to visit national reserves whose purpose is to preserve the plants and animals of the biblical world. The growing population of Israel joins with millions of tourists to create a great deal of stress on these living things. Please stay on the marked trails, refrain from picking plants, and enjoy the wildlife from a distance.

6. *Traditional and Authentic Sites.* Not all sites that claim to have hosted a Bible event did. In some cases the evidence supports the claim. I refer to these as authentic sites. In other cases the connection is less certain. I refer to these as traditional sites. This means that Christians of a later era came to the site to remember a Bible event even though the current evidence may be less supportive of the event actually occurring there. Both traditional and authentic sites have value, but I have favored the treatment of authentic sites in this guide.

page 44 as a guide. Your assignment is to become familiar with the location of five hills, three valleys, and a sixteenth-century wall and its seven gates. Let's start with the topography. Jerusalem of Bible times expanded and contracted around three valleys and five hills. Spend a few minutes with your map and learn the location of the following hills and valleys: City of David, Temple Mount, Western Hill, Mount Zion, Kidron Valley, Central Valley, and the Hinnom Valley. Next, let's add the modern Old City wall. This sixteenth-century-AD wall and its gates are discussed below. For the moment use the map below to see where this wall is located in comparison to the five hills and three valleys mentioned earlier. This map will also help you identify the location of the seven contemporary gates of the modern Old City wall: Joffa Gate, Zion Gate, Dung Gate, Lions' Gate, Herod's Gate, Damascus Gate, and New Gate. Work with this information until you can picture these locations. This will help you build a mental map that you can use to navigate the Old City. And it will help you see how the city of Jerusalem expanded and contracted from the era of King David through the time of Jesus.

With that homework done, let's trace the growth of biblical Jerusalem. David founded Jerusalem on the ten-acre ridge we have identified as the City of David. David's son Solomon expanded the city in order to accommodate a new palace complex and Israel's first temple. His Jerusalem grew to thirty-two acres, a city that enclosed the City of David and the Temple Mount. That is how the city remained until the time of Hezekiah (seventh century BC). He expanded the city to 125 acres by extending the defensive wall of the city to enclose Mount Zion and the Western Hill with a northern wall running approximately from Joffa Gate to Lions' Gate. When the Israelites returned from exile in Babylon during the time of Ezra and Nehemiah, Jerusalem had shrunk back to approximately thirty-two acres and once again consisted of the City of David and the Temple Mount. By the time of Jesus, Jerusalem had grown larger than it had been in any Old Testament era. Herod the Great's Jerusalem was 230 acres. It included all the areas

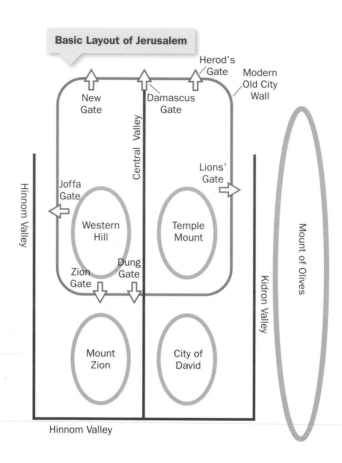

Basic Layout of Jerusalem

Herod's Gate
Modern Old City Wall
New Gate
Damascus Gate
Central Valley
Lions' Gate
Hinnom Valley
Joffa Gate
Western Hill
Temple Mount
Mount of Olives
Dung Gate
Zion Gate
Kidron Valley
Mount Zion
City of David
Hinnom Valley

of Hezekiah's Jerusalem plus a large section that looped northeast of Joffa Gate as far as Damascus Gate before turning south toward the Temple Mount. (To visualize the various stages of Jerusalem, see the illustrations of the city in the time of David, Solomon, Hezekiah, and Jesus on pp. 56, 65, 48, and 52, respectively.)

Akeldama and Hinnom Valley

The Hinnom Valley is a pleasant place to walk. It is a grassy, tree-filled park often full of laughing children playing with their friends. But in an earlier era this valley witnessed some of the most horrific events reported in the Bible, including child sacrifice and the last moments of Judas. Why include this in a visit to Jerusalem? Because only when we appreciate what a sin-ruined heart can do will we fully appreciate the freedom from sin provided by our Savior.

The Hinnom Valley is one of the most heinous historical places in Jerusalem because it is where God's people chose to ignore the first and most important commandment. In the Old Testament, the Lord repeatedly identified himself as the one and only God. He alone deserved the respect and worship of all people. But here Abraham's descendants repeatedly violated this fundamental commandment. They worshiped pagan deities such as Baal and Molech. Unthinkably, some of this worship included the sacrifice of their own sons and daughters (2 Kings 23:10; Jer. 7:31–32; 19:1–6).

This valley is also linked to the death of Judas Iscariot. As you walk east down the Hinnom Valley, look for the Greek Orthodox Monastery of Saint Onuphrius (est. 1874) poised on the southern ridge of the valley. Tradition associates the monastery grounds with the location in which a despondent Judas took his own life. Before his death, Judas attempted to return the money to the chief priest and elders who had hired him to betray Jesus. Disdaining it as blood money, these Jewish leaders quickly used it to purchase a field for the burial of foreigners. It was located in the southern section of the Hinnom Valley and became known as Akeldama, the "Field of Blood" (Matt. 27:3–10).

The Bible paints the Hinnom Valley as an evil place. It feels a bit like that, given its depth and the austere cliffs that line the valley floor. This somber setting invites reflection on the appalling acts of sin and betrayal it hosted. It is a place to remember just how depraved the fallen descendants of Adam and Eve can become. And it is a place to appreciate why Jesus came to Jerusalem the final week of his life. He came to save sinners from eternal death and from the prison of a sin-ruined life. Just a fifteen-minute walk north and uphill from the

Hinnom Valley brings you to Calvary, where Jesus offered himself as the sacrifice for sin, even the kind of sin that once filled this valley.

INFORMATION 📍 descend southwest from Mount Zion and begin your walk in the valley south of the Sultan's Pool adjacent to Gey Ben Hinom Street; 🚫

Bethesda Pools (Saint Anne's Church)

You will find the Bethesda Pools within the compound that includes Saint Anne's Church. Widely regarded as the most beautiful church in Jerusalem, Saint Anne's marks the traditional location of the home of Joachim and Anne. Church tradition remembers them as the father and mother of Mary the mother of Jesus. The Bethesda Pools are adjacent to the church. At these pools Jesus met and healed a man who had been unable to walk for thirty-eight years. (See "Jerusalem at the Time of Jesus" on p. 52.)

Start your visit at the church just right of the entry. The church was built in AD 1140 and remains the best surviving example of Crusader architecture in Israel. Its architects designed the church for chanting rather than speaking. Take a moment to sing slowly here and you will appreciate the wonderful acoustics that carry your voices, filling the building with the sounds of heaven.

The Bethesda Pools predate Saint Anne's Church by eighteen hundred years. These now-dry pools were built to hold runoff water. The northern pool was built during the time of the divided kingdom (eighth century BC). Its builders established a twenty-foot-wide dam across the Beth Zetha Valley to divert runoff water that otherwise would have flowed into the Kidron Valley and been lost for municipal water needs. The second pool was added south of the earlier dam in the second century BC. By the time of Jesus, this double-pool complex had five colonnaded porches to provide shade for those at the pool (John 5:22). Four of the porches lined the perimeter of the double pool, and one went down the middle of the dike.

You may be wondering about the large structures below you in the middle of the pools. These are foundation arches for the fifth-century Church of the Lame Man built to recall the healing miracle of Jesus recorded in John 5:1–15. The main hall of the church sat on the dike, while its flanking aisles extended over the pools, supported by forty-foot arches, one of which can clearly be seen rising from the bottom of the pool.

The Bethesda Pools functioned in three ways. First, they were part of the water-collection system that met the daily needs of those living in Jerusalem. Second, worshipers on their way to the temple grounds used these pools to wash their sacrificial animals. Because God's people brought their animals for sacrifice into the city through the nearby Sheep Gate (today's Lions' Gate), the pools were also known as the Sheep Pools (John 5:2). And third, those with physical disabilities gathered under the colonnaded porches around the pool hoping for a miraculous cure.

This is where Jesus met the disabled man (John 5:1–15). This healing story brings a beam of warmth and hope into Jerusalem. But it also highlights the sorry state of Jerusalem's ordinary residents because it takes place within a stone's throw of the temple. This healing story gives us a taste of the superstition and the unreasonable Sabbath demands that gripped the lives of many. The man Jesus healed believed his only hope for healing would come if someone assisted him into the water when it was stirred. And when Jesus healed this man, the Jewish religious leaders accosted him for carrying his mat on the Sabbath. This is not a world the Lord had designed. Jesus began reshaping the thinking of those who lived near his Father's house by healing the disabled man at these pools on the Sabbath.

INFORMATION
◉ Via Dolorosa Street just north of the Temple Mount;

Broad Wall

King Hezekiah expanded Jerusalem well beyond the city limits established by King Solomon. His Jerusalem stretched to include the Western Hill and Mount Zion. This expansion required the construction of a city wall where none had been before in order to keep those within the city secure. The Broad Wall is a surviving segment of Hezekiah's defensive wall built on the north side of the Western Hill. The austere stones of this wall help us understand the extent of Hezekiah's expansion and give us a look into the heart of this faithful leader.

The story of "good" King Hezekiah is a story of faithfulness to the Lord. Hezekiah called for the elimination of all pagan objects, even those that symbolized the vassal relationship that Israel had with the Assyrian Empire (2 Kings 16:7). This was a righteous act in God's eyes but an act of treason in the eyes of Assyria. Hezekiah knew that the Assyrian army would soon march on Judah to set things straight (2 Kings 18:1–7, 13). Feeling the threat and anticipating a flood

Jerusalem at the Time of Hezekiah

Hezekiah expanded Jerusalem westward across the Central Valley to the sharply defined ridge above the Hinnom Valley.

1 Royal palace of David
2 Spring Tower
3 Pool Tower
4 Siloam Pool
5 Temple
6 Central Valley
7 Kidron Valley
8 Hinnom Valley

of Jewish refugees, Hezekiah revamped Jerusalem's defenses and expanded its defensive perimeter, adding ninety-three acres to the city (2 Chron. 32:5; Isa. 22:10). The segment of this new wall that ran from west to east across the north side of the Western Hill had to be built through a dip in the terrain. To keep the elevation of the wall through this hollow consistent with the wall on either side of it, Hezekiah built the defensive wall higher at this point. And to maintain its structural integrity, he also built it wider. At twenty-three feet wide, it was nearly double the thickness of Jerusalem's wall in other places. The label, Broad Wall, naturally followed and became the name for this portion of Jerusalem's defensive wall (Neh. 3:8).

This archaeology shows the extent of Hezekiah's expansion and offers a powerful faith lesson in stone. The Bible speaks of Hezekiah's expansion of Jerusalem but does not tell us where the city grew. The Broad Wall confirms Hezekiah expanded Jerusalem to include the Western Hill. This became known as the Second District or New Quarter (2 Kings 22:14). But Hezekiah's greatest strength was found not in his wall but in his heart. Faced by an invading army, Hezekiah did all he could. He completed the defensive wall. Then he urged Jerusalem's residents to trust the One who could do more. Believers can follow the model given by Hezekiah when confronted by a challenge in life. We do what we can—and then trust the One who can do more (2 Chron. 32:7–8).

INFORMATION in the Jewish Quarter just north of Hurva Square within a trench surrounded by an iron fence;

Burnt House

Jesus foresaw the future destruction of Jerusalem (Matt. 24:2, 15–21). The Burnt House illustrates what he saw coming. It is a Jewish home/

workshop destroyed by the Romans in AD 70. A multimedia sound and light show interact with the archaeological remains of this house to re-create the horrific final moments of many Jews in Jerusalem that year.

The Burnt House belonged to the Kathros family, one of the aristocratic high priestly families. This segment of Jerusalem's society controlled the business of the temple and was among the elite who built large villas in the Upper City. At the close of the Second Jewish Revolt (AD 132–35), the Romans targeted this portion of the city to make it clear they would not tolerate uprising. As testimony to the Romans' ruthless efficiency, nothing remains of this home but the basement, which appears to have been a workshop for making incense used at the temple.

INFORMATION 📍
Tiferet Israel Street east of Hurva Square; 🚻

To stand in this house is to stand in a moment frozen in time, in the moment of destruction Jesus saw coming on Jerusalem. On the one hand, everything is as it should be. Stone tables and cookware stand at the ready. Even an unused spear leans in the corner where its owner left it. But a closer look shows that nothing is as it should be. Fallen timbers and ash give witness to the violence of this building's last day. And most poignantly of all, the Burnt House displays the skeletal arm of a woman grasping for the stairs as the burning building collapsed around her.

Chapels of Flagellation and Condemnation

The Chapels of Flagellation and Condemnation are both traditional sites. The first recalls the brutal beating of Jesus prior to his crucifixion, and the second recalls the giving of his execution order by Pilate.

The Chapels of Flagellation and Condemnation are in the vicinity of, if not part of, the Antonia Fortress. Herod the Great built this massive, four-towered building on the north side of the Temple

Mount (see "Jerusalem at the Time of Jesus" on p. 52). By the time of Jesus, it had become the barracks for the Roman soldiers stationed in Jerusalem. Was this where Pilate condemned Jesus as tradition recalls? Probably not. It is more likely that Jesus's trial before Pilate and his condemnation occurred at the Palace of Herod the Great on the west side of the Old City, south of Joffa Gate. But it is also very likely that Pilate sent Jesus to the Antonia Fortress so that he could be beaten mercilessly before his crucifixion. This practice of the Romans so weakened the condemned that they offered little resistance when it was time for them to be attached to the cross.

The Crusaders of the twelfth century were the first to erect memorial buildings here. The modern buildings both date to the twentieth century and were built over the remains of those Crusader structures. The artwork within the modern chapels and the devotional setting create a place to reflect on the last hours of Jesus's life. Although it is not possible to identify the exact spot in which the Romans prepared Jesus for execution, this location is in the vicinity. It heard the verbal abuse delivered by the soldiers, the whirr of the slashing whip as it cut through the air, and the groans of Jesus as the blows found their mark. It is a place to read Matthew 27:27–31.

INFORMATION 📍 entry to the chapels' courtyard is in the Muslim Quarter along Via Dolorosa Street; 🚫 🚻

✪ Church of the Holy Sepulchre (Church of the Resurrection)

This is the most important place in the world, the one location in Israel every Christian must visit. The Church of the Holy Sepulchre is where our sin debt was paid. It is where heaven became our home. It is where Jesus died on the cross and rose from the grave.

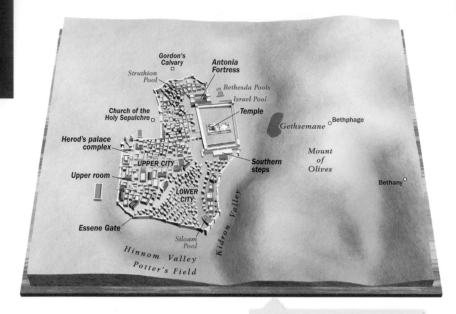

Jerusalem at the Time of Jesus

The location of the church matches every expectation presented in the Bible and assumed by first-century culture (see "Jerusalem at the Time of Jesus"). The church is just outside the first-century wall line of Jerusalem (John 19:20; Heb. 13:12). It was being used as a Jewish cemetery at the time of Jesus's crucifixion, and within the building you can visit tombs that follow first-century Jewish design (John 19:41–42). It is near a public roadway that exited Jerusalem—the kind of location favored by the Romans who wanted public executions to be observed by as many locals as possible. What is more, an unbroken memory lingers around this place. From the first century to this very moment, there has always been a Christian presence in Jerusalem that pointed to this spot as the one that hosted Jesus's death and resurrection.

The relevant history of this location begins in an unassuming way. The area of the church was a rock quarry that provided building materials for Old Testament Jerusalem. When it no longer produced quality stone, the abandoned quarry became a cemetery. At the time of Jesus's trial before Pilate, the Romans used this cemetery as the site for crucifying Jewish criminals, adding more indignity to this undignified form of execution. Jesus was among those criminals crucified here. But unlike other criminals, he was buried here as well in a new tomb prepared for the family of Joseph of Arimathea (John 19:38–42).

After Jesus's resurrection, those who believed came here to worship. Places of worship followed. But the first religious building constructed here was not a church. It was a pagan sanctuary. In the second century AD, the Roman emperor Hadrian sought to change the cultural character of Jerusalem. In response to the Second Jewish Revolt, he drove all Jews from the city, including Jewish Christians. He leveled the old rock quarry where believers in Jesus had worshiped and reconfigured the site as a sanctuary for Venus (AD 135).

That is how things remained for some two hundred years until the Roman emperor Constantine converted to Christianity (AD 312). He sent his mother, Helena, to Jerusalem to establish churches in key locations. Gentile Christians who escaped Hadrian's purge of Jews from Jerusalem pointed her to the pagan sanctuary of Hadrian, indicating that it marked the area of Jesus's death and resurrection. Helena removed the pagan sanctuary and established the first Christian buildings on the spot, dedicated in AD 335. These structures were badly damaged and restored in the years that followed, so that by 1048 only a modest church remained. When the Crusaders came to Jerusalem in 1099, they built a large church on the spot. This building faced damage from earthquakes, fires, and intentional harm inflicted by opponents of Christianity. But it endured. The major components of the current Church of the Holy Sepulchre are those of the Crusader church. Six Christian groups have defined worship spaces in the building: Roman Catholic, Greek Orthodox, Armenian, Syrian, Coptic, and Ethiopian.

There are many things to see in this building; almost all become more specific in tying event to place than a careful review of the evidence allows. The current church building has experienced so much destruction and intentional change that all hope of finding the exact location of the crucifixion or tomb must be abandoned. That has not prevented the pious faithful from doing what the limited evidence has left undone. So what follows is a summary of key locations in the church that tradition has linked to specific moments of Jesus's passion.

Upon entering the current building, you will meet a bewildering maze of rooms, chapels, and artwork. Just inside the main entrance, you will find a slab of marble illuminated by a set of low-slung oil lamps. This is the Stone of Unction or Anointing, the traditional location for the preparation of Jesus's body for burial. Behind the Stone of Unction is a modern mosaic whose tiles add a splash of color to an otherwise dark building. It highlights the final moments of Jesus's earthly life and his burial. Just inside the main entry and before passing the Stone of Unction, a right turn up the steep set of stairs brings you to the highest surviving point of the old rock quarry. This upper balcony with its Latin and Greek Orthodox chapels marks the traditional location of Calvary, the place where Jesus's cross stood. Beneath the glass panels of the Greek Orthodox altar, you can see and even touch a portion of the rock. Returning to the main floor, walk past the Stone of Unction and look for the Tomb of Jesus. This is a small, ornate structure known as the Edicule. This small building constructed within the church replaces the sides and roof of the original tomb of Jesus that were destroyed early in the eleventh century. At the time of this guide's publication, it is undergoing extensive restoration, the first since 1810. There is often a line of those who are anxious to spend just a few moments inside this tomb-like structure. On the back side of this tomb is the small Coptic chapel, which resembles little more than a small closet with an altar within it. Across the hall from this chapel is a dome-shaped room that contains an altar. This is the Syrian Christian chapel. Walk to the far side of this round room and you will find a small, low doorway that leads to a set of first-century Jewish tombs.

During the busier parts of the day when the church fills with tourists, the sanctity of the site suffers. If you are looking for quiet devotional time, try visiting early in the morning or after dinner. At these times, when the quiet is broken only by chanting or the whispered prayers of the Savior's own, the character of the place changes. This may be the best time to read and reflect on Jesus's last moments on earth (John 19:17–20:18). In such moments the church again feels like a sacred site, a place where you can personally connect with the forgiveness of the cross and the joy known in Jesus's resurrection. But the quiet won't last. Soon Christians from all over the world will again press in around you, singing, reading Scripture, and praying in their own languages. This too is an experience worth having. As the church fills with people whose dress and language illustrate the broad geographical scope of the Christian church, it reminds every believer that much of today's worldwide church is made up of people who look very different than the person we see in the mirror every morning.

INFORMATION 📍 given its importance, you might think the church would be easier to find, but it easily blends in with the jumble of buildings around it in the Christian Quarter of the Old City; you will find the church entrance directly off a small courtyard that you can reach by taking Helena Street east from Christian Quarter Road; 🚫 🔄

✪ City of David

The City of David archaeological park preserves the most extensive portion of Old Testament Jerusalem you are able to visit. It includes the birthplace of Jerusalem, two ancient water systems, and homes that show evidence of Jerusalem's destruction by the Babylonians.

Jerusalem at the time of David

Following the civil war that occurred after the death of King Saul, David captured the city of Jebus and its water system. It was then developed into the capital of Israel that was known as the City of David or Jerusalem.

1 Royal palace of David
2 Spring Tower
3 Pool Tower
4 Central Valley
5 Kidron Valley
6 Future site of the temple

This is a large site that involves quite a bit of walking and elevation change if you want to see it all.

Begin your visit at the modern observation tower located at the north side of the City of David. Here you can get oriented and appreciate the challenge David faced when he liberated this spot from the Jebusites. Looking north from the tower, you are looking up toward the higher ridge of the Temple Mount. To the east is the sheer drop into the Kidron Valley that limited Jerusalem's growth in this direction. And beyond that is the extended ridge known as the Mount of Olives. To the south stretches the modest ten-acre ridge that David seized from the non-Israelite Jebusites. This ridge became the first Jerusalem, the capital David established after he had fought a seven-year civil war following the death of King Saul. With the war coming to a close, David needed a secure, centrally located city that could function as a healing capital. The fortified city of Jebus that occupied this ridge was ideal, in part because it had remained in non-Israelite hands and so was neutral during the civil war. With special-forces precision, David's soldiers used the Jebusite water system (discussed below) to gain access to the naturally defended city, whose name was changed to the City of David, also known as Jerusalem (2 Sam. 5:6–10).

Before descending from the tower, consider what Jerusalem meant for the biblical authors and what they expected it to mean for their readers as well. David brought the ark of the covenant here to make his political capital Israel's spiritual capital as well. That means Jerusalem became the place the Lord lived with his people and made himself available to them in special fashion. What is more, Jerusalem is where the Lord Jesus would walk among his people before suffering and dying for their sins. To read the Bible well, we need to join the biblical authors who see Jerusalem as unique among all cities, a place of God's own choosing (Ps. 132:13–14). It is much more than civic pride that shapes the language of Psalm 48 and much more than politics that creates the expectation of Revelation 21. Jerusalem is the Lord's own city, a place to meet him in a more personal way, and a place intimately linked to the hope of forgiveness.

That hope has a great deal to do with what happened in the palace David built after he captured the ridge. You can reach the palace by retracing your steps down from the modern tower and continuing the descent via a set of stairs that leads to the area under the platform of the modern visitor plaza. With this descent, you are entering the palace that King David built (2 Sam. 5:11–12). Little remains of this palace except the foundation. But it is in this "house" that David expressed his desire to build the Lord a permanent "house," that is, a temple. In response, the Lord said he would build David a "house," that is, a dynasty. What is more, the Lord added that the blood of this dynastic family would run in the veins of the long-promised Savior from sin (2 Sam. 7:1–16). This marks the moment that a set of five "ones" becomes fully established, informing our reading of the entire Old Testament. There is one God. There is one nation through whom this one God reveals himself to the world. There is to be one king who rules this nation. There is one dynastic family from which that king is to come. And there is one capital city from which this dynasty will rule, a city that will also house the Lord's sanctuary. These five "ones" center on Jerusalem.

To see the next step in Jerusalem's history, descend via the stairs on the eastern side of the palace. As you walk, note the stepped-stone structure to your right. It predates the time of David's palace; it was used by the builders of the palace as a retaining wall that helped secure the foundation of David's monumental building that rose above it. Continue descending via the steps and think about those five "ones" linked to Jerusalem. You would expect Jerusalem to thrive as a center of worship and theological instruction in support of the one true God. But by the time of Solomon, this son of David built pagan temples for his foreign wives on the southern end of the Mount of Olives, just across the valley (1 Kings 11:7–8). This passion for pagan worship persisted in Jerusalem despite the Lord's repeated warnings. In time the Lord responded. At the base of the stepped-stone retaining wall, you see the price Jerusalem paid for apostasy. The signs provide the names for the dwellings: Ahiel's Home, the House of the Bullae (which contained fifty-one clay seals, or bullae, baked hard by destructive fire), and the Burnt Room. All of these dwellings were destroyed by Babylonian soldiers, the price Jerusalem paid for its unbelief in 586 BC (2 Kings 25:8–12). It is a haunting and moving place to read the grief-stricken language of Lamentations. In its verses you hear the personified city itself grieving over its destruction. The city of hope had become hopeless. "Is it nothing to you, all you who pass by?" (Lam. 1:12).

From here you can descend to the water systems designed to provide secure access to water during times when Jerusalem was under siege. To keep things simple, think in terms of two water systems, one dating from the eighteenth century BC and the other from the eighth century BC. The first is the Canaanite or Middle Bronze water system. It was built long before Joshua led Israel into the land, constructed during the time the Israelites were sojourning in Egypt. The Canaanites (later Jebusites) had built a defensive wall about midway down the ridge. The wall's location took advantage of the natural defenses offered by the terrain but left the Gihon Spring, their water source at the bottom of the Kidron Valley, outside the main defensive wall. In order to secure this water supply, they built two towers. The first was built around the spring itself; it is called the Spring Tower. The second was built around a rock-cut pool that captured the runoff water from the Gihon Spring; it is called the Pool Tower. The early residents of this ridge then dug a tunnel from within their walled city to the Pool Tower, giving them access to fresh water without exposing themselves to the enemy. You can replicate this experience by walking through the tunnel that terminates at the Pool Tower. In this area the massive stone foundations of both the Pool and Spring Towers are evident, towers whose walls are as much as twenty feet thick.

If you prefer to keep your feet dry, this is the time for you to exit via the dry tunnel. This is part of the eighteenth-century-BC water system that allowed water to flow to the gardens in the Kidron Valley. Once outside, you can follow the signs leading downhill toward the Shiloah (Siloam) Pool. On this walk you will pass a quarry with two large openings that some have associated with the royal tombs of the house of David.

If you are ready to get your feet wet and have brought along a flashlight, it is time to explore Hezekiah's Tunnel (eighth century BC). But you need to know several things about this walk: the tunnel is unlighted and shoulder-width, averages less than five feet in height, and requires you to walk in water up to thirty-two inches deep.

This tunnel was built by King Hezekiah in preparation for the arrival of the menacing Assyrian army. They were headed his direction because Hezekiah's religious reforms had destroyed symbols of the treaty Israel had made with Assyria. Knowing that trouble was on the way, Hezekiah expanded Jerusalem from 32 to 125 acres. But this additional room for refugees also signaled the need for water in amounts that the old system could not provide. The Central Valley

The Siloam Inscription, which was removed from Hezekiah's Tunnel and now resides in the Istanbul Archaeological Museum in Turkey. It tells of how the tunneling crews could hear each other shout as the two excavating teams got close to one another. The tunnel's shape shows that they adjusted their route to compensate.

provided the solution. As Hezekiah expanded Jerusalem, he enclosed this valley within the city walls. The low elevation of its southern reach created the ideal spot to build a water reservoir to capture and hold water. But to get water into this reservoir from the Gihon Spring, it was necessary to dig a tunnel from the bottom of the Kidron Valley, through the City of David ridge, to the Central Valley where the reservoir was located. The urgency of the moment meant that two excavating teams set to work, tunneling from each valley toward the other a hundred feet underground. They must have followed some natural feature in the stone until they were close enough to hear each other's pick blows. An inscription dating to the time of construction, the Siloam Inscription, tells part of this story. After as many as three years of work, the mining teams met and the water flowed (2 Kings 20:20; 2 Chron. 32:30). As you walk the tunnel, imagine the urgency of the work and the frustration of the many false starts you will see along the way as the two teams frantically edged toward the meeting point.

After you exit the tunnel, you will come upon a small pool. This is the traditional Pool of Siloam built by Christians in the fifth century to recall the miracle Jesus performed in John 9:1–11. Jesus met a man born blind, applied mud made with his saliva, and directed him to wash in the pool. After the man washed, his sight was restored. Continue past the traditional pool, walk up and down another set of stairs, and you will come to the authentic Pool of Siloam to which Jesus sent the man born blind.

You are now in the very bottom of the Central Valley, and it is time to end your visit at the City of David. For a small fee it is possible to catch a shuttle back to the City of David plaza where your visit started. Alternatively, it is possible to walk back up the City of David ridge by using the black cobblestone driveway and walkways that make the steep climb back to your starting point. A third option is to use the recently discovered first-century street and Central Valley drainage system, which will again put you underground until you exit the passageway near Dung Gate.

> **INFORMATION** 📍 walk south and exit the Jewish Quarter using Dung Gate; then walk east for about half a block before turning right on a narrow street that leads to the visitor entrance; 📖

Ecce Homo Convent of the Sisters of Zion

The Ecce Homo Convent derives its name from an ancient arch incorporated into its architecture, the Ecce Homo Arch. *Ecce homo* is the Latin expression "here is the man," the statement made by Pilate at Jesus's civil trial (John 19:5). Christian tradition has linked the civil trial of Jesus to this area, and so the Latin expression became linked to the arch and the convent.

The arch, the large water cistern (Struthion Pool), and the "stone pavement" within the convent all date to about one hundred years after the death of Jesus and were built by the Roman emperor Hadrian. That means the Stone Pavement identified as the site of Jesus's trial (John 19:13) is not the same stone pavement within the Ecce Homo Convent. You would do better to seek the place of the civil trial of Jesus before Pilate and the Stone Pavement mentioned in John in the Palace of Herod the Great, located south of Joffa Gate. Nevertheless, the space occupied by the convent is connected to the last hours of Jesus's life. The convent is located in the area of the four-towered Antonia Fortress. By the time of Jesus's trial before Pilate, this building had become a barracks for the Roman soldiers. After Pilate conducted Jesus's civil trial, he likely sent Jesus to the Antonia Fortress to prepare him for execution (Matt. 27:27–31; Mark 15:16–20; see "Jerusalem at the Time of Jesus" on p. 52).

Although the stone pavement of the Ecce Homo Convent is a different pavement than the one mentioned in John 19, it contains something that may have been related to the soldiers' mocking of Jesus. A game board incised into the rocky paving stones is known as the King's Game. This was a dice game played by the Roman soldiers whose winner was crowned king. The scarlet robe, crown of thorns, staff, and disdainful language of the Roman soldiers may well have been a form of this game that they used to mock the royalty of Jesus, which they believed to be as much a sham as the homage given to the winner of the King's Game.

INFORMATION 📍 the convent and arch are located north of the Temple Mount on Via Dolorosa; 🕧

Garden Tomb (Gordon's Calvary)

The Garden Tomb is a traditional location linked with the crucifixion of Jesus and his resurrection from the dead. Its relatively quiet setting and peaceful garden provide a more relaxed environment for worship and reflection than the Church of the Holy Sepulchre. But the latter is the authentic location for these world-changing events.

The first time you will find a connection made between the Garden Tomb and Jesus is the middle of the nineteenth century. A short time later, in 1883, the British general Charles Gordon claimed the site as the Protestant alternative to the Church of the Holy Sepulchre. When he looked at the side of the hill included in this garden park, Gordon saw eroded features that resembled the eye sockets, nose, and mouth of a human skull. Although these features are much less prominent today, they were clear enough at the time of Gordon to lead him to the conclusion that this was Golgotha, "the place of the Skull" (John 19:17; see "Jerusalem at the Time of Jesus" on p. 52). For Gordon, the hill was the place of Jesus's crucifixion, and the tomb at its base was the site of Jesus's burial and resurrection. There is no doubt that the cave in the side of the ridge is a tomb. But the architecture of the tomb dates it to the era of the Old Testament (800–600 BC), removing it as a candidate for the "new tomb" of Joseph of Arimathea.

While the evidence linking this site to the death and resurrection of Jesus is relatively late and tenuous, the Garden Tomb endures as a place for quiet meditation and worship. The Church of the Holy Sepulchre (the more likely setting for Jesus's death and resurrection) is so cluttered by church art, tradition, and people that many Protestants find it an unsatisfying location to reflect on the event in history that most profoundly changed human destiny. But here in the relative quiet of this very aromatic garden, you can enjoy a peaceful atmosphere that invites worshipful reflection and prayer.

INFORMATION 📍 after exiting Damascus Gate, take Nablus Road north one-quarter mile and then turn right on Conrad Shick Street; 🚫 free tours of the site are available.

⭐ Jerusalem Archaeological Park

The Jerusalem Archaeological Park preserves and reconstructs a portion of New Testament Jerusalem walked by the most notable individuals we meet in the New Testament, including Mary, Jesus, and Paul. Begin your visit in the Davidson Center, where a multimedia presentation will introduce the historical and cultural context of this park, which preserves the southern and southwestern approaches to the temple in Jerusalem.

Walk east and then south to the far end of the park to see the oldest structure in the complex, a gate built at the time of King Solomon. When Solomon expanded Jerusalem to the north across the natural dip in the terrain (Ophel) between the City of David and the Temple Mount, he built a gate into the eastern part of the wall that provided access to the Kidron Valley. The foundation of Solomon's gate, seen here, continued to serve this role at the time of Nehemiah when it was called the Water Gate (Neh. 3:26).

Retrace your steps north from this gate and you will travel uphill into the Herodian architecture of Jesus's day (see the illustration "Herod's Temple Complex" on p. 82). The broad stairway ahead is known as the southern steps or rabbi's teaching steps. This was the main public entry and exit for the temple. Look for the more rustic-looking stairs in the lower sections of the reconstructed staircase—these are the stairs that date to the time of Jesus. Most modern stairs are built symmetrically. As you walk up these stairs, you will discover their irregular pattern. Unlike modern stairs, these require the user to exercise greater concentration. This is by design. The architects wanted every worshiper to think carefully about the walk they were taking toward the temple, the place in which God made his presence known in a special way.

Jerusalem at the time of Solomon

Solomon expanded Jerusalem to include the ridge immediately north of the City of David, more than doubling the size of the capital city of Israel.

1 Royal palace of David
2 Spring Tower
3 Pool Tower
4 Palace complex of Solomon
5 Temple
6 Central Valley
7 Kidron Valley
8 Solomon's gate

As you walk the stairs, think of those who walked here before. Jewish society converged here in the first century. Three times a year, families made their way to Jerusalem for the three major festivals that required a visit to the temple. That means notable characters of the New Testament like Elizabeth, Mary, the twelve disciples, Paul, and Jesus walked these very steps.

Two specific New Testament stories are likely to have occurred here. Luke tells us that when Jesus was twelve years of age, he stayed behind in Jerusalem after his parents had left for home in order to learn more about the Scriptures and the mission his heavenly Father had set for him (Luke 2:40–52). After exhausting the understanding of his parents and the rabbi in Nazareth, Jesus turned to the leading Jewish educators of his day, educators who lived in Jerusalem and often met their students on these stairs.

This is also the most likely setting for Peter's Pentecost sermon (Acts 2:14–40). It provided the open space needed to gather thousands, was the natural gathering point for the diverse Jewish crowd with whom the disciples spoke, and offered the necessary acoustics that allowed so many to hear the gospel that day. At the close of the sermon, those who received Jesus as their Savior sought baptism (Acts 2:41). Look just to the east of these stairs and you can see the foundations of a building that contained Jewish traditional bathing stations (*mikvaoth*). These pools, some with divided stairs, offered the opportunity to complete the required preworship ritual bath. They also would have provided water for some of the baptisms that followed Peter's sermon. And here is one more thing to think about. During that sermon, Peter mentioned you. He said that the promises linked to Jesus were "for all who are far off—for all whom the Lord our God will call" (Acts 2:39).

The main entry and exit doorways that worshipers used to gain access to the temple courtyards are silhouetted in the stone wall behind the bath station. These doorways led to ramps that climbed to the temple courtyards above you. Let your eyes move east down the wall above the stairs and you will see the outline of a triple gate (now filled in). Look closely at the west side of this entry and you will see an ornately carved stone doorjamb that dates to the time of the New Testament. The second gateway is located on the same stone wall but farther to the west and is partially obstructed by a later medieval wall. It too is filled in. Look above the modern window and you will be able to pick out a long horizontal block that spans the opening of the doorway stone with an arch of small stones above it. These are elements of the first-century doorway.

When you have finished your time at the southern steps, walk back toward the entrance of the park, pass through the doorway in the later-period wall, and look for the right turn that leads to the southwestern corner of the Temple Mount. This is the best location to get a sense of the massive retaining wall needed to hold up the Temple Mount platform. The temple proper resided on a hill with the terrain falling in elevation to the south. To create a level platform for worshipers near the temple, ancient engineers cut away bedrock north of the temple and added fill to compensate for the decreasing elevation of the terrain to the south. The massive stones before you were quarried, moved, shaped, and then laid without mortar to become the retaining wall that holds the fill in place.

Above you on the retaining wall, you will see stones that project to form the base of an arch. The arch above your head would have crossed the valley floor and connected with the massive foundation stones just to your west to form Robinson's Stairway. This L-shaped staircase connected the pedestrian walkway in the Central Valley with the Royal Stoa, a multistory structure that extended the full width of the Temple Mount's southern side. The openings in the bottom of the staircase, together with the small arched structures opposite them along the retaining wall base, provided discrete space for dozens of shops. The sidewalk that traveled under the arch and north along the western side of the retaining wall was a shopping mall.

Just north of the arch, you are sure to notice the large tumble of stones. These stones come from New Testament–era structures that had been built on top of the Temple Mount. In response to the First Jewish Revolt, Rome made a point of attacking the very heart of Jewish identity, the temple complex. The large stones now resting on top of the shopping street had been part of the buildings and balustrade, a barrier that prevented an accidental fall from the top of the Temple Mount platform. Roman soldiers demolished those structures and levered them over the edge of the Temple Mount platform in AD 70, a stunning fulfillment of Jesus's words: "Not one stone here will be left on another; every one will be thrown down" (Matt. 24:2).

Before you leave this area, walk to the base of the wooden stairs to the south and look for a stone whose top was carved into a gentle curve. The stone was part of the balustrade that guarded the upper edge of the Temple Mount. This particular stone was special because it contained an inscription: "To the place of trumpeting." When the clergy sounded the shofar (ram's-horn trumpet) from here to mark the start and end of the Sabbath (as well as mark other important times), its echoing call could be heard throughout Jerusalem. The original inscription is now in the Israel Museum, but look up and you can see the original location of this stone on the south-

INFORMATION

⦿ in the Old City just north of Dung Gate;

west corner of the temple complex. Here is where Satan likely tempted Jesus (Matt. 4:5–7). Had Jesus stepped off this corner of the Temple Mount and gently floated to earth before hundreds of shoppers, his popularity would have surged. But Jesus made it clear that he would have nothing to do with obtaining a kingdom without the cross.

✪ Kidron Valley Overlook

The Kidron Valley Overlook offers exceptional views of the Kidron Valley and the Mount of Olives. As Bible readers we meet the Kidron Valley under a variety of names and circumstances. It is the Valley of

Shaveh or the King's Valley where Abram met Melchizedek. It echoed with the righteous hammer blows of reformers like King Hezekiah and King Josiah who were bent on destroying pagan imagery. It knew the steps of Jesus as he walked between Jerusalem and Bethany. And it is the Valley of Jehoshaphat, which provided the context for the longest discourse Jesus gave on the end times.

The geographical importance of the Kidron Valley is hard to over-state. Its sharp profile provided Jerusalem with natural defenses on its eastern side, and its deep cut into the surface of the earth created Jerusalem's two natural water sources, the Gihon and En Rogel Springs. In addition, the Kidron Valley becomes part of the travel corridor between Jerusalem, the Mount of Olives, and the wilderness beyond. The natural route travels the valley floor and then over the Mount of Olives through the dip in a ridge just north of where you are standing. David used this road when he was fleeing Jerusalem ahead of his son Absalom (2 Sam. 15:23), and Jesus would have repeatedly used this route as he moved between Bethany and Jerusalem during Holy Week.

Three monuments will catch your eyes in the valley below. The square-based structure with the bottle-shaped roof is called the Tomb of Absalom. This monument was cut from the rocky cliff in the first century BC, much later than the time of Absalom. Nevertheless, in the twelfth century it was identified with the monument that Absalom built for himself in the King's Valley (2 Sam. 18:18). A second square-based structure but with a pyramidal roof stands just south of Tomb of Absalom. This second tomb, also carved from the rocky cliff, is likewise given a name it does not deserve: Zechariah's Tomb. It was built in the second century BC, long after the time of Zechariah's death. The final structure, the Tomb of the Sons of Hezir, is the only one whose popular name has an authentic connection to Bible history. This is the square opening before you marked by its two Doric columns. The architecture of the tomb indicates that its construction dates to the first century BC. However, an inscription on the stonework above the columns links the tomb to the Hezir family. This is a priestly family with an Old Testament heritage (1 Chron. 24:15).

The writers of the Old Testament mention the Kidron Valley as the place where divine judgment is delivered. Kings Asa, Hezekiah, and Josiah destroyed pagan worship aids here (1 Kings 15:13; 2 Kings 23:4, 6, 12; 2 Chron. 29:16). The prophets saw the final judgment of the world occurring here. Joel says the nations will be gathered to the Valley of Jehoshaphat for judgment (Joel 3:2, 12), and later Zechariah speaks of the messianic judge gathering the nations to Jerusalem as he stands on the Mount of Olives (Zech. 14:2–5). Jesus had a tendency to select specific locations to enhance his teaching. He chose this location for the sustained conversation with the disciples on the end times (initiated in Matt. 24:1–3).

This link to the final judgment explains the presence of all the tombs in view. Jews, Muslims, and Christians all believe that this will be the place of resurrection and judgment, so all three faith traditions have cemeteries here. The southern end of the Mount of Olives is filled with Old Testament Jewish tombs, some of which are visible under the homes in the modern Arab village of Silwan on the ridge to your right. A modern Jewish cemetery with more than ten thousand graves fills the Mount of Olives ridge just north of Silwan. This is complemented by a Christian cemetery in the valley floor and Muslim tombs just below the Old City wall behind you.

A place of burial and divine judgment in the past becomes a place for reflecting on the divine judgment to come. Jesus spoke about the end times here, and he ascended into heaven from the top of the Mount of Olives near the thin tower of the Chapel of Ascension. All of that makes this a meaningful place to reflect on the close of our own lives as well as the return of Jesus. You can do that by reading and reflecting on the end-times lesson Jesus taught here, found in Matthew 24–25.

Old City Wall and Gates

Only in a place as old as Jerusalem is it possible to think of a sixteenth-century wall as "modern." Suleiman the Magnificent, a Turkish sultan, completed the modern Old City wall by 1541. He used the wall to define his Jerusalem, and it in turn defines the Old City of Jerusalem found within the 2.7-mile wall Suleiman built. The current wall is cut by eight gates, seven ancient and one modern. On the west is Joffa Gate. On the north are New Gate (1887), Damascus Gate, and Herod's Gate. On the east are Saint Stephen's Gate (Lions' Gate) and the walled-up Golden Gate. On the south are Dung Gate and Zion Gate.

Is this the same wall as the one Jerusalem had in Bible times? Yes and no. The continuity is evident in the western and eastern segments of the wall. The western segment from Joffa Gate to the wall's southwest corner follows a rocky outcropping that hosted the wall of Jerusalem from the eighth century BC (the time of Hezekiah) to the middle of the sixth century BC, when Babylon destroyed Jerusalem. By the time of Jesus, Jerusalem's western wall was again following this rocky outcropping. However, in both eras the western wall would have continued south beyond the point at which the modern wall turns east. The biblical wall continued south to the campus of Jerusalem University College and only then turned east. On the eastern side of the city, the modern Old City wall marks the location of the Old and New Testament walls of Jerusalem, starting at Saint Stephen's Gate and moving south. But once again the city wall of Bible times would have traveled past the point where the modern Old City wall ends. It would have continued so as to include the City of David ridge.

There is another way in which the Suleiman Wall is the same wall as the one of biblical Jerusalem—its stones. Biblical Jerusalem faced destruction and renovation many times during its history. When new walls were built, there was no need to quarry new stones

when the stones of earlier walls could be reused. The same is true for the building of the modern Old City wall. Its stones may have been changed in shape and location, but ponder this: touch any stone in the modern Old City wall, and there's a good chance you are touching a stone that was part of the wall of Jerusalem during events we read about in the Bible.

Saint Peter Gallicantu

The modern Catholic church of Saint Peter Gallicantu (Latin for "cockcrow") claims to reside where Caiaphas's home once stood, the home in which Caiaphas interrogated Jesus and in which Peter denied his connections with Jesus three times (Matt. 26:57–75; John 18:12–27). The golden rooster on top of the building recalls the cockcrow that followed Peter's third denial.

The modern church rests on the foundation of an earlier fifth- to sixth-century-AD Christian structure. Given Crusader evidence from the twelfth century AD, it seems more likely that early Christians came here because they believed it to be the place to which Peter fled after denying Jesus, the place he wept with bitter remorse (Matt. 26:75). If you are looking for the authentic location of Caiaphas's home, it may be within the Armenian Church of Saint Savior on Mount Zion. Byzantine visitors from the fourth century point us in this direction.

Nevertheless, a visit to Saint Peter Gallicantu has something to offer. It is a quiet location that provides a wonderful view of the three valleys above which biblical Jerusalem grew. On the grounds you will find a small model of Byzantine Jerusalem. The Byzantine Christians erected many churches in Jerusalem. Consequently, the model is very helpful for orienting yourself to how those buildings first looked and where they were located. These buildings include the sprawling Nea Church, the Church of Holy Zion, and the Church of the Holy Sepulchre.

But the most moving place on the campus for Christian visitors is the set of ancient steps that descend from this property toward the Siloam Pool. These steps date to the first century AD and provided access to the Kidron Valley and the Mount of Olives. When Jesus left the upper room and traveled to the Garden of Gethsemane and when he returned to Mount Zion bound for the home of Caiaphas following his arrest, his feet likely touched these very stones. Imagine the thoughts that filled his mind as he faced the horrible close to his life that became the ultimate solution for sin in our own.

INFORMATION 📍 outside the Old City walls on the southeastern side of Mount Zion; 🚻 🏛

Temple Mount (Haram esh-Sharif)

The Temple Mount is the artificial platform on which the Jewish temple resided and on which worshipers gathered around the temple. Today it is home to the Dome of the Rock, the third-holiest place in Islam. Ever since the Six-Day War of 1967, when the Old City of Jerusalem became part of the modern state of Israel, control of the platform has remained with leading Muslim clerics in conjunction with an agreement between them and the state of Israel. The clerics, together with the Israeli police, control access to and behavior on the Temple Mount.

The current platform reflects the expansion of this worship plaza at the time of Herod the Great, when it grew to thirty-six acres to accommodate the increasing number of worshipers coming to the temple (see

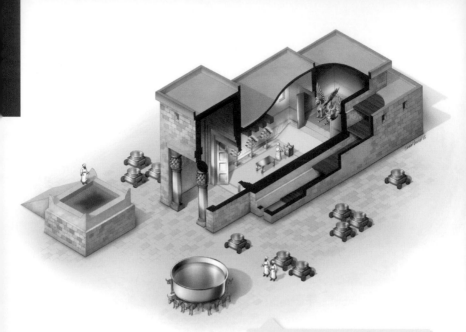

Solomon's Temple

Solomon built a temple for the Lord in Jerusalem that had the same floor plan, worship furnishings, and rites as the earlier tabernacle (1 Kings 5–7). But while the tabernacle was a portable tent, the temple was a permanent stone structure (90 feet long and 30 feet wide).

the illustration "Herod's Temple Complex" on p. 82). In Herod's day the platform was filled with lavish architecture. Because God made his presence known in a special way here, those soiled by their own sin faced increasing restrictions as they approached the Holy of Holies. These restrictions are reflected in labels like Court of the Women (the area beyond which the women could not go) and Court of the Gentiles (the area beyond which gentiles could not go). To prevent gentiles from accidently advancing farther than they were allowed, the platform included a four-and-a-half-foot wall that defined the Court of the Gentiles. On the north, east, and west sides of the platform, rows of pillars held up the roofs of shade porches that surrounded the plaza. These colonnaded porches were a natural place for visitors to gather and so a natural place for Jesus, Peter, and

John to speak with them (Matt. 21:15, 23; 26:55; Acts 2:46; 5:20–25, 42). And at the heart of it all was the holy temple. What remains of this magnificent architecture for you to see? Nothing but a few large paving stones.

The most striking building on the platform today is the Dome of the Rock, one of the most iconic symbols of Jerusalem. Its golden dome, composed of gold electroplated on copper, has a warm, natural glow at dawn and dusk. Muslims erected the first building on this site in AD 691 because they believed it marked the stone from which Mohammad rose on his night journey to heaven. For Jews and Christians, this building marks the summit of Mount Moriah, the location of Araunah's threshing floor, which David obtained and over which Solomon built the first Jewish temple (2 Sam. 24:18–25; 2 Chron. 3:1). Although the shape of the temple was different than that of the Dome of the Rock, the current building can help you appreciate the size of Solomon's temple. The temple was built on the same location, with a front porch that rose sixty feet higher than the Dome of the Rock. The Babylonians destroyed this temple in 586 BC. But this first temple was followed by a second temple (515/516 BC) built in the same spot by the exiles who returned from Babylon. Herod the Great enhanced the Second Temple complex, but shortly after it was finished the Romans destroyed it in AD 70. Unfortunately, nothing of these temples remains in view.

On the south side of the platform, you will see the Al-Aqsa Mosque. It marks the area of Herod's Royal Stoa (Royal Porch). This monumental, ten-story building ran east–west across the top of the southern wall of the Temple Mount. It had the floor plan of a tall basilica built with 162 columns, each four and a half feet in diameter. These pillars divided the long hall of the basilica into three long aisles with a semicircular apse at one end. From time to time the Jewish Sanhedrin met here. And this was the location of the temple markets that Jesus addressed so forcefully during his last week in Jerusalem (Mark 11:15–18).

Travel to the northwest side of the platform and you will see a rock outcropping on which the Muslim Umariyya School now stands. In the New Testament era, this rock was the foundation of the four-towered Antonia Fortress, which allowed the Roman soldiers to keep a watchful eye on the Temple Mount. This area on the northwest side of the platform hosted the events described in Acts 21:27–22:23 that led to Paul's arrest, his trial in Caesarea Maritima, and his journey to Rome.

> **INFORMATION** You must pass through a security station and present your passport. Hours are limited. Generally, access is possible Monday through Thursday for just a few hours in the morning and afternoon. You must dress very modestly. You will not be able to enter the buildings on the plaza. You will be prohibited from taking your Bible or other religious study materials with you. You are required to refrain from open worship and from discussing topics other than the Muslim history of the site. 📍 access for non-Muslims is through the Moor's Gate via a ramp located north of Dung Gate; 🚫 👕

Tower of David Museum (Citadel)

The Tower of David Museum presents a brief history of Jerusalem starting with its founding at the time of David and continuing through the modern era. Of particular interest is the archaeology in its courtyard, including surviving components of Herod the Great's palace, which in its day extended from the museum grounds to the southwest corner of the modern Old City wall.

The Tower of David carries a name it does not deserve. Byzantine Christians thought this hill was part of the City of David and so presumed that the ruin of the large tower belonged to David's palace, hence the name Tower of David. However, the large square stones at the base of the massive tower are part of the palace complex erected here by Herod the Great (see "Jerusalem at the Time of Jesus" on p. 52). Herod built a luxury palace in Jerusalem acclaimed by the first-century historian Josephus as "wondrous beyond words" (*Jewish War* 5.176). On the north side of the palace where the natural defenses were the weakest, Herod built three towers: Hippicus (120 feet tall, named for his friend), Phasael (135 feet tall, named for his brother), and Mariamne (85 feet tall, named for his wife). Most consider the Tower of David foundation to be the foundation of the Phasael Tower.

Follow the signs that lead from gallery to gallery to get an overview of Jerusalem's history from the Old Testament era into the modern times via artifacts and exhibits. Be sure to get a panoramic view of Jerusalem's Old City and its surroundings from the observation deck on the top of the tallest tower. Then drop into the open-air courtyard, where a maze of foundation walls runs through a lovely garden. Let your eyes run along the wall segments marked as belonging to the Hasmonean and Herodian eras and you will be tracing the arching, northwest wall line of Jerusalem during the New Testament era. If you are looking for some evening entertainment, the museum offers a sound and light show (the Night Spectacular) that presents Jerusalem's history by projecting virtual reality images on the ancient walls of the citadel.

INFORMATION
📍 in the Old City just inside and south of Joffa Gate; 🅱

⭐ Upper Room

The Upper Room, also known as the Cenacle or the Coenaculum, is a traditional location that commemorates the place Jesus ate his last meal with the disciples, the Passover meal that became the Lord's Supper or Eucharist (see "Jerusalem at the Time of Jesus" on p. 52).

But this is just one of three important events linked to this room. During his lectures given in AD 348, Cyril, bishop of Jerusalem, said that the room in which Jesus initiated the special meal known as the Lord's Supper was also the place where Jesus made his postresurrection appearances to the disciples (Mark 14:14–15; John 20:19, 26). He added that this was the very room in which the disciples sat as the day of Pentecost began (Acts 1:13; 2:1–2).

This collection of important events, all associated with the upper room, made it a place worth remembering, and a series of buildings were constructed for that task. After the original home and its upper room were destroyed by the Romans in response to the First Jewish Revolt (AD 70), Jewish believers in Jesus constructed a public building on the site, perhaps a Jewish-Christian synagogue. European Christians incorporated this structure into the Church of the Apostles (fourth century AD) and then into the Holy

On Maundy Thursday, Jesus and the disciples likely reclined around a low table like this in the upper room. Each took a position around the table that related to the social role they played during the meal and to their social status among those dining together.

Zion Church (fifth century AD). The Persians destroyed this church in AD 614, and Crusader-era Christians built a new church here using building materials from earlier eras. This means that the Upper Room you are visiting is not the same room in which Jesus and the disciples met but rather the upper room of a fourteenth-century building that uses some architectural components of the twelfth-century Crusader church. One other twist in history is necessary for you to understand the Islamic elements of the room. When the Turks arrived in 1524, they converted the room into a mosque designed to honor the prophet David. (Byzantine tradition had inaccurately associated the location of the upper room with the tomb of King David.)

It can be difficult finding a quiet moment to reflect on the collection of events that have drawn Christians to this spot for more than two thousand years. After visiting the Upper Room proper, you may find the peace you seek by taking the stairs that lead to the roof of the Upper Room. Here, away from the crowds, you can more easily reflect on the powerful things that happened here, events that impact your life on a daily and eternal basis. Jesus initiated the Lord's Supper here, a meal that marks the transition between the Old and New Testaments and speaks words of forgiveness in our lives. Jesus met the disciples here and offered convincing proof that he had risen from the dead, proof that animated their confidence and led them to boldly preach the gospel. And this is where the miracle of Pentecost began, a day that ended with the conversion of thousands and the start of the gospel's journey to the far corners of the world, including our own.

INFORMATION 📍 second floor of a building adjacent to the Dormition Abby on Mount Zion; the entry is directly across from the modern statue of King David playing a harp; 🚫

Via Dolorosa

The Via Dolorosa (Way of Sorrows) is the traditional route Jesus walked in the final hours of his life, leading to the culminating moments of his death and resurrection. The current fourteen stations mark key moments at the close of Jesus's life (most historical but some based on later tradition), such as his condemnation by Pilate, his speaking to the women of Jerusalem, and the place of his crucifixion. Many Christians make this devotional walk in order to reflect on the meaning of these last hours of Jesus's life for them.

The first record we have of individuals making this walk dates to the time of the Byzantine Christians, who brought the idea to Jerusalem from Europe. On Maundy Thursday, the night Jesus was betrayed and arrested, they walked from the Eleona Church on the top of the Mount of Olives to Gethsemane, and then to the Church of the Holy Sepulchre. This meaningful experience became a tradition, but the route and the number of stops repeatedly changed from the fourth to the nineteenth century. By the time of the eighth century, devotional stops were added that became known as the "Stations of the Cross." In the fourteenth century there were eight stations. The current route with its fourteen stations (five of them within the Church of the Holy Sepulchre) took shape in the nineteenth century.

Although the current Via Dolorosa ends in the correct location, at the Church of the Holy Sepulchre, the majority of the route does not follow the actual last path of Jesus. That is because the current route still reflects an earlier understanding of where these events occurred and the travel limitations imposed on Christian visitors during Islamic control of the city. While this may compromise the experience for the purist, the devotionally minded who wish to thoughtfully and prayerfully walk the Old City will find the Via Dolorosa a meaningful experience.

✪ Western Wall (*HaKotel*)

The Western Wall (known in Hebrew simply as *HaKotel*, "the wall") is the most sacred spot on earth for the observant Jewish community and is arguably the most Jewish location in the world. It is an outdoor synagogue where it is possible to see the modern Jewish community worshiping near the spot on which the Old Testament temple stood.

To appreciate what you are seeing at this location, you must know what the Western Wall was and what it is for those who come here to worship. It was a retaining wall built in the time of Herod the Great. As the need for level space near the temple proper increased to accommodate a growing number of worshipers, the worship plaza around the temple grew in size. Creating a level platform meant trimming away stone from the ridge that lay north of the temple and adding fill to the south of the temple where the terrain decreased in elevation. The latter task required the construction of retaining walls to hold the fill in place. The Western Wall in front of you is part of the retaining wall that made the thirty-six-acre plaza possible (one of the largest *temnos* plazas in the ancient world). When the Romans destroyed the temple in AD 70 in response to the First Jewish Revolt, they destroyed everything on the plaza but did not destroy the lower courses of this retaining wall. Consequently the retaining wall is the one element of the first-century temple complex that remains. Given the legacy of these stones and their proximity to the temple (which was located where the Dome of the Rock now stands), Orthodox Jews come to worship

Herod's Temple Complex

1 Ritual bathhouse (*mikvaot*)
2 Southern steps
3 Robinson's stairway
4 Barclay's gate
5 Western Wall
6 Wilson's bridge
7 Royal Stoa
8 Solomon's Porch
9 Court of the Gentiles
10 Soreg
11 Court of the Women
12 Nicanor Gate
13 Temple
14 Antonia Fortress

and pray here. Even though this was merely the retaining wall holding up the platform on which the temple sat, they believe the divine presence never left this wall. That is why they come to worship here and why they reverently back away from the Wall at the close of their visit.

The Western Wall is a place to appreciate ancient craftsmanship of Herod the Great's builders. Approach the wall and notice the carefully executed design of the stones and the precise way each stone mates with its neighbors. This masonry is dry laid (without mortar), which requires that each stone be carefully chiseled to precise dimensions. In the Wall on the south side of the outdoor women's synagogue, you can see the twenty-foot-wide lintel of a doorway called Barclay's Gate. This partially visible doorway was another entry to the temple complex. On the northern side of the underground section of the men's synagogue, you will encounter a massive arch known as Wilson's Arch. This arch (and its companion, which can be seen by walking north from the Western Wall plaza up al-Wad Street) provided the foundation for a bridge that spanned the Central Valley between the Western Hill and the Temple Mount.

The Kotel Plaza is also a place to respectfully watch the observant Jewish community in worship, because here you will get a taste of how the Jewish community of the Old Testament must have looked to those who were not Jewish. The Lord had always asked his chosen people to dress, act, and worship in ways that were unique, reminding them and others of their special relationship to the Lord and distinctive responsibilities. Worship at the temple was one of those markers. When the temple was destroyed, observant Jews put even more emphasis on the other cultural markers of their Jewish heritage. A Monday or Thursday visit will make these markers particularly apparent. These are bar mitzvah days, when young boys go through a religious initiation that marks them as adults responsible for observing the religious obligations of their faith. Friday at sunset is also a good time to visit. This is when the plaza comes alive as worshipers welcome the arrival of the Sabbath with lively dancing and singing.

Finally, this is a place to worship. Go to the wall and thoughtfully read the prayer Solomon offered at the dedication of the first temple (2 Chron. 6:13–42). And take time to read Hebrews 10:1–18, a comparison of Jesus's sacrifice to the ones performed at the temple. These readings are meant for this place and may well lead you into prayer. If

INFORMATION All visitors must go through security similar to that at an airport checkpoint. Respectful recording of your visit with photographs is permitted on all days except during Sabbath. Because certain portions of the plaza are regarded as an open-air synagogue, men and women must separate if they wish to go to the wall proper, men to the left and women to the right. ⦿ northeast side of the Jewish Quarter below the Dome of the Rock;

you chose to do so, you can join the thousands who have written out a special prayer and placed it in a crack in the wall, leaving it before the Lord, whose presence surely lingers here.

Wohl Archaeological Museum

The Wohl Archaeological Museum preserves the remains of six multistory homes in which the wealthy elite of Jerusalem lived at the time of Jesus. This included the aristocratic priests or Sadducees who built their palatial homes on the top of the Western Hill in the Upper City of Jerusalem (see "Jerusalem at the Time of Jesus" on p. 52). These are the homes that the ordinary folks of Jesus's day would never see; but you can. In doing so you will learn a bit more about the Sadducees. The visit will also provide you with insights into the experience of Peter, who denied knowing Jesus in just such a home.

Jesus interacted with the Sadducees during his time in Jerusalem and had a hearing before the high priest in just such a home. But the Gospel accounts give few details about the Sadducees. That is where the evidence in this museum becomes valuable for Bible students. Here you can get an idea of who the Sadducees were and what was important to them. Pay particular attention to the design and surviving contents to see how dramatically their lives differed from the ordinary people of the land. While ordinary families lived in single-room homes with simple furnishings and dirt floors, these folks enjoyed spacious homes (the largest was over six thousand square feet) whose design included large reception halls, open-air courtyards, private baths, private ritual baths (*mikvoth*), mosaic floors, stucco walls designed to simulate marble, and walls painted with geometric figures (frescos). Their contents include foot washing basins (see John 13:5) and lathe-turned stone jars (the kind that did not transmit ritual impurity; see John 2:6), in addition to stone tables and dishware.

The last and largest of the homes encountered during your visit to the museum is particularly indicative of the home of the Jewish high priest. Its floor plan may help you understand Peter's threefold denial of Jesus at the time of Jesus's hearing before the high priest (John 18:15–19). It is safe to say that Peter had never been in such a home. It was large, with a complicated network of rooms and hallways. In the middle of it all was a large, enclosed courtyard. As a Galilean used to a simpler life and a much simpler home, you can appreciate how the architecture of this building must have confused Peter and made him feel trapped. Although he may have wanted to leave after his first denial of Jesus, he likely did not know the way out! It does not excuse his actions, but it will help you understand how the architecture of the high priest's home may have contributed toward his denial of Jesus.

INFORMATION

southeast side of Hurva Square in the Jewish Quarter;

2

Jerusalem and Beyond

Drivable Sites outside the Old City

⭐ Bethlehem and Shepherds' Fields

It is always Christmastime in Bethlehem. Singing "Silent Night" in April or "O Little Town of Bethlehem" in August sounds out of place anywhere but here. In Bethlehem, we recall one of the great miracles of all time—the eternal God was born as a baby. Mary and Joseph tucked Jesus into an animal's feedbox. And the heavenly Father dispatched angels to deliver a birth announcement like no other. Who can keep from singing Christmas songs in such a place! Now it is your turn.

The singing of Christmas music in Bethlehem, just a short drive from Jerusalem, has a very long history. The current Church of the Nativity

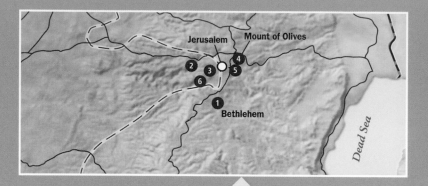

1 Bethlehem and Shepherds' Fields
2 Ein Kerem
3 Israel Museum
4 Mount of Olives
 · Chapel of the Ascension (Mosque of the Ascension)
 · Church of All Nations (Basilica of Agony)
 · Dominus Flevit
 · Mount Scopus Observation Point and First-Century Tomb
 · Pater Noster Church (Eleona Church)
5 Rockefeller Museum
6 Tisch Family Zoological Gardens

sits on top of what remains of a cave. Ever since the second century AD, local Christians have pointed to this cave as the animal shelter in which Mary gave birth to Jesus (Luke 2:4–7). Long before the first building graced the site, Christians gathered here. This got the attention of the Roman emperor Hadrian (AD 135), whose goal was to eradicate all worship not directed to the Roman gods. He converted the site into a pagan worship complex. Ironically, this helped preserve the memory of the spot until the time of the Christian emperor Constantine. Helena, the mother of Constantine, built the first Christian church here (AD 339). From the fourth century to the present moment, the cave's location has been marked by a Christian building.

The building you are about to visit contains a few elements of the fourth-century church but is most closely connected to its sixth-century replacement. The architecture tells its story. As you look toward the church from Manger Square, your eyes will catch the small, square doorway that is the church's entry. Above this small entry, which dates to the sixteenth century, you will see two others that are now filled in.

The middle opening with a pointed arch was built for the Crusader church, and the larger squared-off entry served the church built by the Christian emperor Justinian in AD 539. He is the one who tore down the fourth-century building and replaced it with a much larger place of worship. The footprint of the current church and its major architectural components date to this era, making it the oldest Christian church in the Holy Land. It survived when other churches did not because of a piece of artwork. The marauding Persian invaders (AD 614) destroyed all the Christian churches in the promised land except this one. Christian tradition says they spared this church because of a piece of artwork on the façade depicting the magi. Because the people in the artwork resembled them, the Persian attackers spared the building. While this piece of sixth-century art has not survived, some fourth-century mosaics have. This is something you will not want to miss. As you enter the main building, look under the large wooden doors on the floor and you will find beautiful mosaics that adorned the floor of the church built by Helena. In 2013, restoration of the church's wall mosaics began. These extensive mosaic murals are among the best you will see on your trip to the Holy Land. They made their public debut in 2016. After you have seen these, walk to the right of the ornately decorated Greek Orthodox altar area and look for a set of semicircular stairs. These lead to the Grotto of the Nativity. This highly decorated space is what is left of the birth cave of Jesus. Tradition has marked the place of birth with a fourteen-point star and marked the location of the feeding trough in which Mary placed the infant with a facsimile manger.

Immediately adjacent to the Church of the Nativity is the Roman Catholic Church of Saint Catherine. A statue of Saint Jerome greets you in the courtyard. And lest you pass by him without a thought, realize you have something in common with this noted scholar of the past. He believed that geography was important to Bible reading. As the translator commissioned to bring the message of the Bible into the common language of his day, Jerome produced the Latin Vulgate.

In Judea, where caves are plentiful, many built their home over a natural cave. It provided a basement for storage and a shelter the family's livestock. The upstairs was divided into a larger living area for the family and a narrow guest room, which could be offered to relatives who were traveling.

Knowing how much geography there was in the Bible, he moved to the Holy Land to be sure that he got that part of his translation right. His office and tomb lie beneath the Latin church. Descend by a set of stairs located on the right side of the sanctuary to visit them.

Bethlehem is a busy, noisy place. If you are in need of a quiet place to gather your thoughts, take the short drive east to the city of Beit Sahour to visit the fields tradition has linked with the Christmas shepherds (Luke 2:8–20). At the Franciscan Shepherds' Fields, Byzantine Christians established a religious compound to remember the angelic birth announcement. And thankfully its devotional character is unchanged. A pine-scented path leads toward the modern church. Here in a lovely garden you will find natural caves like those that were pressed into service as animal shelters. Unlike the cave in the Church of the Nativity, these still look like caves! Opposite the caves, you will find a metal walkway that leads into the ruins of a Byzantine monastery. This is the best place on the grounds to get some quiet time.

As you read the Christmas story (Luke 2:1–20; Matt. 2:1–13) and sing your favorite Christmas songs, think about the relationship of these events to those in the Garden of Eden. Once Adam and Eve had fallen into sin, everything changed. For the very first time, they felt the need to hide from their Creator. The joy and peace they had known in the Lord's presence was replaced by fear (Gen. 3:10), the fear that every sinner feels when standing in the presence of holiness. The shepherds felt it too on that first Christmas. They were terrified when a holy angel appeared to them and the glory of the Lord shown around them. But that reaction was out of place this night, and the angel addressed it before saying anything else: "*Do not be afraid.* I bring you good news that will cause great joy for all the people" (Luke 2:10; emphasis added). The very first words spoken by Adam and Eve after the fall into sin were words of fear. The very first words spoken by the Lord to mortals on the first Christmas were "Stop being afraid." That is what the birth of Jesus means for every sinner.

> **INFORMATION** 📍 travel south on Highway 60 from Jeru-
> salem and watch for the signs directing you to the Bethlehem
> checkpoint; both Bethlehem and Beit Sahour are in the West Bank
> outside the modern state of Israel, so you will need to bring your
> passport to secure entry and exit; 🚫

Ein Kerem

The village of Ein Kerem is not mentioned by name in the New Testament, but early Christian tradition linked it with the home of Zechariah and Elizabeth, the parents of John the Baptist.

Two modern churches invite a few moments of your time. The Church of John the Baptist is a nineteenth-century church built over ruins of an earlier Byzantine church. It is distinguished by its tall tower and orange roof. This Franciscan church surrounds the cave believed to be the birthplace of John the Baptist. Across the village lies the Church of the Visitation. The façade of this twentieth-century church is adorned by a mosaic that recalls the visit Mary made to her cousin Elizabeth after she had received the news that she would be the mother of Jesus. Without language more specific than this, we read that Mary traveled to meet Elizabeth in a "town in the hill country of Judea" (Luke 1:39).

This is the place to take out your Bible, to read, and to reflect on the song of joy that came to Mary's lips during her visit. The song is known as the Magnificat (Luke 1:46–55). It shows just how much Mary had grown since the day she struggled to understand what the angel Gabriel had announced to her in Nazareth, and it is rightly regarded as one of the most powerful pieces of inspired poetry in the Bible. Ein Kerem is also a wonderful spot to read the story of John the Baptist's birth (Luke 1:5–25, 57–80), which includes Zechariah's song of celebration, known as the Benedictus. This song, which takes only a minute or two to read, captures the centuries of waiting that God's people experienced as they watched for the Messiah to be born. Both songs remind us of something critical to the well-being of the church. The Lord regularly uses the most ordinary of people from the most ordinary places to accomplish extraordinary things.

INFORMATION 📍 southwest side of modern Jerusalem near the modern Hadassah hospital; 🚫

Israel Museum

Jerusalem hosts many museums, but leading the pack is the world-class Israel Museum. Its sprawling campus and expansive collection of art, archaeology, and Judaica will consume more than a full day for the most avid of museum visitors. Here we will focus on those elements of the museum that are of greatest interest to Bible students.

Start your visit outside at the scale model (1:50) of first-century Jerusalem. The designers have combined archaeological discoveries and ancient literary descriptions of Herodian Jerusalem to construct this three-dimensional model of the city. While walking in Jerusalem itself, you can see bits and pieces of first-century Jerusalem. But here you can see the city as Jesus would have known it with the temple complex, Palace of Herod the Great, Upper City, and Golgotha.

Your eyes will be drawn to a large white dome as you walk the museum campus. This is the Shrine of the Book, the museum dedicated to the Dead Sea Scrolls, Jewish literature dating from the second century BC to the first century AD. The roof of the building is shaped like the cover of a ceramic vessel, the kind of vessel in which the famous scrolls were discovered. Inside, you can trace the history of the scrolls (starting with their discovery in 1947), see examples of the scrolls themselves, and learn about their value. Among the scrolls are some of the earliest examples we have of the Hebrew Bible, and they help us secure more precisely the wording of the Old Testament Hebrew text that lies behind our English translations. In addition, they add to our understanding of the Jewish culture that Jesus encountered and addressed during his earthly ministry.

Reserve the bulk of your time for the archaeology wing. The deep history of this land is laid bare in this expansive collection of man-made items. These artifacts offer compelling insights into the way people lived and thought in this special land. You will find things like a four-horned altar from Beersheba; the Tel Dan Stela, which contains the earliest extrabiblical mention of David's dynasty; the Ketef Hinnom silver scrolls, which contain the oldest written portion of the Old Testament; a seat of Moses from Capernaum; Tyrian shekels like those provided by the money changers at the temple; and the ossuary (secondary burial box) of Caiaphas. The collection is organized by historical period, so be sure to have the timeline included in this guide on hand to help you link the collection with Bible history.

> **INFORMATION** 📍 in the western portion of modern Jerusalem in Givat Ram, off of Ruppin Road; 🚌 (see www.imj.org.il).

⭐ Mount of Olives

The Mount of Olives is a two-mile-long ridge that lies east of Jerusalem's Old City. Although it was never included within the defensive walls of Jerusalem in either the Old or New Testament era, it has always been connected to the city. The less fertile southern portions of the ridge became the city's cemetery, and the fertile northern slopes hosted commercial olive groves. Today Christian chapels dot the ridge, recalling events from the last hours of Jesus's life. Because it is several hundred feet higher than the Old City, the Mount of Olives offers the best panoramic views of ancient Jerusalem, which photographs best in the morning light.

Chapel of the Ascension (Mosque of the Ascension)

The ascension of Jesus took place on the Mount of Olives (Luke 24:50–51; Acts 1:6–11). Today a seventeenth-century mosque, which replaced a Byzantine church, marks the traditional spot of this dramatic event.

Early Christian pilgrims to the land mention a church associated with the ascension of Jesus. But there are no remains of this church to be seen. One seventh-century pilgrim described a round building that surrounded a stone in which the footprint of Jesus could be seen, the last footprint he left on this earth before ascending into heaven. Others added that the center of this chapel was unroofed so that its worshipers could look up into the heavens as the disciples did on the day of Jesus's ascension. When the Crusaders arrived, they replicated the architecture of this earlier chapel. A portion of that building is evident in the central courtyard of the mosque. Approach

INFORMATION
📍 Rub'a el-
Adawiya Street in
At-Tur; 🌓 ⛰

the circular chapel in the courtyard and look closely at the columns adjacent to the filled-in arches. On top of those arches, you will see capitals making the architectural transition between the top of the pillar and the arch above. The most ornate of these capitals date to the Crusader era.

★ Church of All Nations (Basilica of Agony)

Jesus led the disciples to the Garden of Gethsemane following the Passover / Lord's Supper meal, where he struggled in prayer, faced the betrayal of Judas, and was arrested (Matt. 26:36–56). The specific location of the garden that hosted these events on the Mount of Olives is not known. But the most accessible of the traditional locations for these events is the Roman Catholic Church of All Nations.

The entry of the church compound leads directly into a beautiful garden that contains many old olive trees like those that filled the original Garden of Gethsemane. Just how old these trees are is difficult to tell because olive trees do not have a set of concentric growth rings like other trees. However, carbon dating of the oldest trees here indicates they date to the twelfth century AD.

The modern church (1924) beyond the garden is built above the foundation of its fourth-century predecessor. The design of the modern church re-creates the atmosphere of the fateful evening of Jesus's struggle in prayer with its dark-purple windows and a black ceiling adorned with painted stars. The ceiling also contains twelve seals commemorating donations from the twelve nations that contributed to the modern church's construction (hence its modern name, Church of All Nations). Three mosaics dominate the interior and direct our attention to the front of the church. In the center and just above the large rock that tradition defines as the rock on which Jesus struggled in prayer is a depiction of Jesus on that rock. To the left and right are mosaics depicting Jesus's betrayal and arrest.

The church is meant for quiet reflection and worship. Its atmosphere creates the opportunity for you to think about the stunning decision Jesus made that evening in the Garden of Gethsemane, a decision he made only after pursuing his options with the heavenly Father in prayer. Read Matthew 26:36–56. Do we hear Jesus speak like this at other times in his life? Faced with his death and the thoughts of bearing the penalty for the sin of all sinners of all time, Jesus was looking for an alternative. And what is more, his location on the Mount of Olives presented him with an escape option. He could have dashed into the Judean Wilderness that lies just east of the Mount of Olives. Within a mere forty minutes, he could have been in the same trackless wilderness that offered David isolation from Saul. This walk was in Jesus's own best interests. But thankfully it is a walk he did not take. Instead, he turned back to the disciples and walked down the path toward the arresting party, only to be led back into Jerusalem and to the cross. Only when Jesus makes this turn away from the wilderness can sinners breathe a sigh of relief. It is literally the difference between eternal life and death. Let that inform your time in prayer here where Jesus prayed.

INFORMATION 📍 east of the Temple Mount on the lower flanks of the Mount of Olives; it is distinguished from other churches near it by the large and brightly colored mosaic on the façade that depicts Jesus accepting the punishment for sinners; entry to the compound is on El-Mansuriya Street 🚫 ⭕

⭐ Dominus Flevit

Dominus Flevit (a Latin phrase meaning "the Lord wept") is the traditional location recalling the moment Jesus wept over Jerusalem as he approached the city on the first Palm Sunday (Luke 19:41).

The church compound contains a first-century cemetery and highly decorated ossuaries. Look for them just after entering the gate to the compound under a stone shelter to your right. The architecture of the first-century tomb is hard to make out, but the ossuaries are not. An ossuary is a limestone box that Jews of the first century used to collect the bones of family members who had been previously buried.

The architecture of the main building recalls the tear-filled experience of Jesus. Its modern Roman Catholic chapel was completed in 1955 and built over the footprint of a fifth-century-AD Christian monastery chapel and its mosaics. The modern building is shaped like a tear drop. It has four tear vases located on the four corners of the roof, replicating vessels that first-century families used to capture their tears of grief upon losing a loved one to death.

This location, although slightly south of the route Jesus used to enter Jerusalem on Palm Sunday (Matt. 21:8–11), is the best place to reflect on the relationship between the language of those who welcomed Jesus that day and the place where that welcome was given. Those who cheered Jesus's arrival were ready for a coronation. Their language recorded in the Gospels makes that clear: "Hosanna to the Son of David!" "Blessed is the coming kingdom of our father David!" "Blessed is the king!" (Matt. 21:9; Mark 11:10; Luke 19:38). The motivation for this coronation language was geographical. Those welcoming Jesus that day observed him descending into the Kidron Valley on the back of an animal headed in the direction of an ancient spring. They saw a repeat of Solomon's coronation. This son of David had ridden an animal provided by his father down into the Kidron Valley to be crowned king of Israel at the Gihon Spring (1 Kings 1:32–35). Now they saw Jesus, the son of

David, riding an animal provided by his Father into the bottom of the Kidron Valley in the direction of that same spring. The geographical symmetry naturally led them to use coronation language.

> **INFORMATION** 📍 midway down the west side of the Mount of Olives; you can choose to either climb or descend the steep street that extends from the Mount of Olives observation point (above the large Jewish cemetery) to the Church of All Nations; 🚫 🏛

⭐ Mount Scopus Observation Point and First-Century Tomb

The Mount Scopus Observation Point offers striking views of the greater Jerusalem area, and the first-century tomb located below the observation platform provides an opportunity to readjust your image of the tomb in which Jesus was buried and from which he rose on Easter Sunday.

This portion of the Mount of Olives goes by the name Mount Scopus. As the name suggests, it is a mountain with a view. The higher elevation of this plaza and its unobstructed view make it one of the best viewpoints for capturing the larger geographical context of Jerusalem and for photographing the Old City.

Just below the plaza you will find the ruins of a first-century Jewish tomb. This is the style of tomb built by well-to-do Jewish families of Jerusalem from 20 BC to AD 70. That makes it the type of tomb that Joseph of Arimathea would have built for his family. And that makes it the kind of tomb in which Jesus was buried. Although both the roof and original entrance of the tomb are missing, enough of the architecture survives to illustrate the nature of the tomb that provided the setting for the Easter Sunday story (Matt. 27:57–28:15; Mark 15:42–16:8; Luke 23:50–24:8; John 19:38–20:18).

The story of Jesus's burial sounds just like you would expect a Jerusalem story of the first century to sound except for the wonderful

When Joseph of Arimathea offered his tomb for the burial of Jesus, it was likely a *kokhim*-style tomb. The main room of the tomb had a bench around its perimeter, which was to prepare the body before placing it in one of the smaller *kokhim* (niches). In twelve to eighteen months, the family would return to the tomb, gather the remains from the *kokh*, and place them in a limestone box called an ossuary.

interruption caused by Jesus's resurrection. Following Jesus's death, Joseph of Arimathea gained custody of Jesus's body so that he and others could respectfully bury it, thus fulfilling Isaiah 53:9. They took Jesus's remains to Joseph's new tomb and laid it on the preparation bench, one like the large three-surface bench that lies in the middle of the tomb before you. Here they washed and then lovingly wrapped Jesus's body with linen strips, inserting aromatics between the layers. The setting of the sun marking the start of Sabbath interrupted this process, so they left Jesus's body on the preparation bench. They intended to return after Sabbath to complete this process of preparing Jesus's body for burial and then place his body into one of the small chambers inset into the walls on the perimeter of the tomb. The Hebrew name of the chamber is *kokh*.

(There are multiple chambers like this hewn in the tomb because it was designed for the burial of multiple family members.) According to expected Jewish practice, the body would have remained in the *kokh* for twelve to eighteen months until the tissue decayed, leaving only the bones. The family then would return to the tomb, remove the bones of their loved one from the *kokh*, and place them in a limestone box called an ossuary. The bones would remain in the box, and the box would remain in the tomb awaiting the great resurrection.

When Jesus's disciples and friends began to arrive on Easter Sunday morning, nothing was as they had left it on Friday. Jesus's body was no longer on the preparation bench, only the linens in which they had wrapped it. The *kokh* awaiting the body lay empty. The unnatural appearance of things demanded a supernatural explanation, one that the Lord provided when he sent his angels with this message: "He is not here; he has risen, just as he said. Come and see the place where he lay" (Matt. 28:6).

INFORMATION 📍 parking area and plaza southwest of the Hebrew University campus on Binyamim Mazar Street; 🚫

Pater Noster Church (Eleona Church)

The Pater Noster Church has enjoyed a steady stream of Christian visitors since the third century AD, but not all of them came for the same reason. A third-century document, the *Acts of John*, spoke of a cave located on the Mount of Olives in which Jesus taught the disciples. The first visitors thought the cave located in the church courtyard was that cave. Early in the fourth century AD, Helena (mother of the Christian emperor Constantine) constructed her Eleona Church here. She did so believing that the area of the cave was also the setting for Jesus's ascension. (Later that same century, Christian pilgrims reported worshiping at another chapel closer to the highpoint of the ridge that was associated with Jesus's ascension. This became the Chapel of the Ascension mentioned above.) By the twelfth century AD, the focus of attention again shifted to the cave. In particular, Christians recalled this as the spot Jesus taught the disciples the Lord's Prayer (Matt. 6:9–13; Luke 11:2–4). This is the Crusader tradition that has persisted to the present time and that led to the building of the current Pater Noster Church. (*Pater noster* are the first two words of the Lord's Prayer in Latin.)

You can do a number of things in this compound. You can visit the cave that tradition has linked to Jesus's teaching of his disciples. You can visit the 1920s church that is a partial reconstruction of the fourth-century church built here by Helena. But the most striking feature in the compound is the presentation of the Lord's Prayer in dozens of languages on ceramic plaques throughout the cloister (covered walkways). Here we feel the broad sweep of the Christian faith shared by people from all corners of the world as reflected in the languages they use to worship in their home churches. You can do here what believers in Jesus have done for thousands of years: find a quiet place and give voice to the prayer Jesus gave as a model to use in shaping our prayers.

INFORMATION 📍 E-Sheikh Street on top of the Mount of Olives, just south of the Chapel of the Ascension; 🔹 🔹

Rockefeller Museum

John D. Rockefeller Jr. provided significant funding for the construction of the museum that bears the Rockefeller name. The growing number of artifacts unearthed in the region during the early part of the twentieth century needed a home, and this museum provided it. In the 1930s it quickly became the premier museum of Jerusalem. Beyond the artifacts, the architecture of this museum is something of a historic curiosity worth seeing in its own right. Compared to other modern museums, the Rockefeller represents a step back in time with its distinctive white, octagonal tower and its tall, echo-prone galleries that host wooden display cases.

The antiquities within date from the prehistoric era to about AD 1700. The curators have arranged the collection chronologically, allowing visitors to move to the galleries of greatest interest to them. While the Rockefeller sports a more modest collection of artifacts than the sprawling Israel Museum, it does contain several unique treasures: intricately carved ivory pieces from Late Bronze Canaanite Megiddo, a number of the Lachish letters written in the sixth century BC just prior to the Babylonian captivity, eighth-century-AD decorative wooden panels from the Al-Aqsa Mosque, and the elaborately carved lintels that hung above the entry of the Crusader-era Church of the Holy Sepulchre.

INFORMATION 📍 in East Jerusalem outside the Old City walls just northeast of Herod's Gate; 🚫

Tisch Family Zoological Gardens

The Tisch Family Zoological Gardens (also known as the Jerusalem Zoo) provides a very different experience from the museums and archaeological parks of Jerusalem. Animals both large and small surrounded those living in this land in Bible times—from the powerful Syrian bear to the graceful Persian fallow deer to the soaring short-toed eagle. The biblical authors, like everyone else in Bible times, spent most of their lives outdoors. As they walked from place to place, they came into contact with animals like these. They observed them, came to know their habitats, and learned their habits of living. So it is not surprising that the biblical authors mention these animals and presume that their readers will have an understanding of their habitat and habits as well. This experience is hard to recover today because habitat loss and a growing human population have driven these animals from the land or forced them to find refuge in places most visitors will not travel. Aside from the ubiquitous hooded crows and laughing doves of Jerusalem, many visitors will leave Israel without meeting most of the animals mentioned in the Bible. For those who would like to learn more about these wonderful creatures, there is no better place to begin than with the Tisch Family Zoological Gardens. This zoo, which sprawls over sixty-two acres of hillside, wishes not only to preserve the species that had been part of this land but also to educate its visitors about their habitat preferences and habits. Signs provide the basic information and include Bible connections.

INFORMATION southwest of the Old City of Jerusalem near the Jerusalem (Malcha) Mall on Derech Aharon Shulov Street;

3

Coastal Plain

As the name suggests, the coastal plain is the sloping plain that extends along the full length of Israel's Mediterranean coastline, interrupted only by the so-called antelope's nose of Mount Carmel. In contrast to the mountains to the east, this is a gently rolling landscape that travels well, farms well, and invades easily. Although the coastal plain enjoys some of the best real estate in the region, the Israelites rarely inhabited it and almost never controlled it. Consequently, you will find very few Bible events and very little of the Bible's communication linked to the coastal plain.

Ashkelon

Ashkelon was an ancient harbor and trading center that enjoyed ready access to fresh water and agricultural fields. A variety of peoples

1 Ashkelon
2 Caesarea Maritima
3 Haifa
4 Jaffa (ancient Joppa)

exploited this port city that was a bridge between overland trade routes and maritime ship-
ping, including the Canaanites living here at the time of Abraham's
family, Egyptians at the time of Joshua, Philistines at the time of David,
the Romans, and the Crusaders.

Ashkelon lacked natural defenses, so the Canaanites built a substantial rampart (a massive earthen berm) around their 150-acre city,
one of the largest in this region. (Compare that to the average Israelite
town, which was a mere seven acres in size.) To gain an appreciation
for the city defenses, stop at the Canaanite Gate parking area on the
north side of the park. Here you will see the largest surviving section
of the Canaanite defensive rampart that stood between attacker and

city. Imagine the challenge faced by an attacking soldier who had to run up this fifty-foot-high rampart while facing attack from above. During peacetime, access to the city through the rampart was via a gatehouse. The weight of the material above the entry would have collapsed the doorway if it had been built using a more conventional rectangular shape. Instead, the force lines of the heavy superstructure were redirected around the entry using a series of arches made of stone and sun-dried mud bricks. Thanks to the conservation efforts of archaeologists, you are able to walk through this reconstructed gatehouse, one of the oldest arched gates in the world. It dates to approximately 1850 BC.

Ashkelon almost always belonged to someone other than Israel during Bible times (Josh. 13:3; 2 Sam. 1:20). From 1200 to 600 BC (the time of the judges through the time of the divided kingdom) it belonged to the Philistines. That makes this a good place to think about their influence on Bible history and grow in appreciation for their power. This Aegean people brought advanced metal-working skills and weaponry with them when they migrated to this region. As a result, they displaced the local Canaanites as the ruling elite. Their presence constantly menaced Israel. In response, the elders of Israel demanded that Samuel appoint a king to rule over them (1 Sam. 8:4). Both Saul and David, the first two kings appointed by Samuel, regularly battled the Philistines as they sought to establish a successful monarchy in Israel. Watch for their mention in the Bible, particularly in regard to the power they projected from their five city-states, including Ashkelon (1 Sam. 5:1; 7:7; 13:16–18; 17:4; 2 Sam. 5:17–18). The Philistines were no ordinary opponent. So when the Lord gave Israel victory over them, it was a big deal. That reality forms part of the backstory to the well-known events of 1 Samuel 17, the story of David and Goliath. During his subsequent rule, David restricted the influence of the Philistines but did not deal them a final blow. That came at the hands of the Babylonian Empire just as Jeremiah 47 announced.

INFORMATION 📍 on the beachfront of the Mediterranean Sea just southwest of the modern city of Ashkelon; 🅱️

⭐ Caesarea Maritima

Herod the Great loved the art and culture of Europe. So this Middle Eastern king needed a seaport to connect him with Rome and its luxury goods. Caesarea on the sea was his answer. Herod built this 165-acre city, flush with imported architecture and building materials, between 22 and 10 BC. What is more, Herod designed this city to have a thoroughly European look and feel. To be in first-century Caesarea was like being in Rome, even though you never left the Middle East. Caesarea National Park preserves the essential elements of this Herodian city as well as Byzantine and Crusader architecture that followed.

Start your visit on the south side of the archaeological park where you can enter the reconstructed four-thousand-seat theater. The location of the theater, its general design, and components like the marble paving stones in the orchestra floor are original. Realize that a theater like this was essential for making Caesarea a truly Roman city. The theater in a Roman city was not just an entertainment venue but also an instrument for communicating the beliefs and ideals of Greco-Roman culture. It had as much influence on its citizens' worldview as the imperial temple that Herod dedicated to his patron, Caesarea Augustus, built just above the harbor.

To the north of the theater on the seashore, you can walk through the footprint of Herod's palace. This was a multistory residence that Herod used for entertaining his guests. The design plan included a garden courtyard surrounded on all sides by a continuous porch lined with columns. Guest rooms lay just beyond the porch. To the west, guests could enjoy an ornate swimming pool and accompanying patio. When Herod died, Rome began to rule Israel with European governors, men like Pontius Pilate who used this city as the regional seat of government. Pilate, Felix, and Festus all called this palace home. While they spent time in Jerusalem as necessary, they lived in Caesarea, which had the amenities and feel of their European homeland.

A few more steps north will bring you to Herod's hippodrome. This was the venue for an ancient form of NASCAR racing that involved horse-drawn chariots pulled at breakneck speeds around an oval track. Sadly, this was also the setting for the execution of many who took part in the First Jewish Revolt against Rome (AD 66–70). In the second century AD, the hippodrome was moved and the complex refashioned to form an enclosed amphitheater in which art and sport were celebrated, sport that included gladiatorial events.

The crowning architectural achievement of this city was its deepwater harbor. You will find its remains north of the hippodrome. The ancient harbor included not only the area of the modern harbor but also the green lawn near the ancient arched warehouses. The arrogance of Herod is clearly laid bare in this project. He was determined to build this harbor in a location known for its dangerous shoals, requiring a complete reconfiguring of the natural landscape. He established breakwaters (one 1,800 feet long and the other 600 feet long) to define the inner harbor and then dredged the seafloor to allow larger ships access to this artificial bay. The foundation of these breakwaters employed hydraulic cement (cement that hardens under water). This engineering innovation had never been used to the extent that it was here. One of the ingredients for this cement was *pozzolana*, volcanic ash found in Italy. In order to complete the project, Herod imported forty-four shiploads of this ash at four hundred tons per ship. When it was finished, Caesarea Maritima boasted a harbor more than twenty-five acres in size, the second largest in the ancient Roman world. In AD 130 a devastating earthquake dropped the seafloor in this area, taking all evidence of this first-century harbor below the waves. Study of the ancient harbor continues with archaeologists who use scuba gear to study its underwater remains.

The substantial city that grew up around this harbor faced another major challenge. There was insufficient freshwater here to meet the needs of its population. As a result, Herod constructed a water delivery system that brought water thirteen miles from the base of Mount Carmel to the city, half of that distance in channels and the other half on a raised aqueduct. The sea has taken its toll on this water delivery system, washing most of it away, but you can visit a surviving segment just north of the archaeological park. After exiting the Crusader gate on the north side of the park where the Crusader era wall and moat are most evident, follow the signs guiding you on the short drive north to the sandy beach.

Both Peter and Paul spent time in Caesarea Maritima, fifty-four miles northwest of Jerusalem. It was a place that changed them both in fundamental ways. Through a series of visions, the Lord called Peter to leave the more Jewish seaport of Joppa for Caesarea Maritima in order to speak to gentiles about Jesus. This was a big step for a Jewish man who saw gentiles as unclean. How much worse that Cornelius was a representative of the occupying Roman army! This was a cultural obstacle that the early church needed to cross. In gentile Caesarea the Lord showed Peter that everyone, even someone like Cornelius, was eligible for kingdom membership. These gentiles received the Holy Spirit and were baptized just like the Jewish believers in Jerusalem on the day of Pentecost (Acts 10:1–48). This gentile Pentecost was something Peter could not keep to himself. He quickly traveled to Jerusalem and told the Jewish-Christian church that a gentile Christian church was alive in Caesarea Maritima. In the end, this Caesarea story changed the church. After hearing it, Jewish believers in Jerusalem concluded, "So then, even to Gentiles God has granted repentance that leads to life" (Acts 11:18).

Caesarea Maritima changed Paul too. He embarked from this seaport on his journey to Rome, but only after the Lord allowed him to remain in detention here for two years (Acts 23:31–33; 24:27). If you are puzzled by the delay, consider what Caesarea had to offer Paul. He knew the Jewish way of life and the Jewish faith. But if he were going to travel to Rome and advocate for Jesus in that European setting, Paul had to come to a better understanding of how Europeans thought and did their politics. Caesarea Maritima was Rome away from Rome. There was no better place for Paul to get to know Europe while still in the Middle East. So the Lord kept him in this setting for two years and enhanced his understanding of the Roman world. Then, when the time was right, Paul made his emboldened plea to be heard before the emperor (Acts 25:1–12). Caesarea then provided him with one last thing, the harbor from which he could set sail for Rome.

INFORMATION 📍 on the Mediterranean Sea coast near modern Caesarea; 🅿️

Haifa and Israel's Ancient Maritime Culture

Haifa hosts the main seaport of the modern state of Israel. If you are interested in ancient maritime culture, two museums in the museum-rich city of Haifa beg for your attention: the Hecht Museum and the National Maritime Museum.

Hecht Museum

The curator of the Hecht Museum has organized artifacts like coins, seals, and oil lamps chronologically from the time of Abram through the Byzantine era. However, the display you may find most interesting is titled "The Phoenicians on the Northern Coast of Israel in the Biblical Period." Phoenicia, Israel's neighbor to the north, enjoyed natural deep-water seaports and timber resources that favored the development of a ship-building and maritime-trading culture. These advantages gave the Phoenicians something special to offer ancient Israel in exchange for what Israel could offer, agricultural products. This exchange of food for maritime expertise took place during the rules of David, Solomon, and Ahab. For example, Hiram, king of Tyre, built Solomon's navy and provided lessons in maritime commerce (1 Kings 9:26–28; 10:22; 2 Chron. 8:18).

The Greeks who came to the promised land during the time between the Old and New Testaments also had a maritime culture. The museum has one of their ships called the Ma'agan Mikhael Ancient Ship. This display presents a 2,400-year-old Greek merchant ship and a portion of its cargo.

INFORMATION

📍 on the campus of Haifa University; 🚫

National Maritime Museum

This museum has a seven-thousand-item collection dedicated to the history of shipping in the Mediterranean Sea. That allows for a quite complete presentation of the harbors, shipbuilding, and maritime commerce on the Mediterranean Sea. The displays include maritime mythology, old merchant maps, models of ships, navigation equipment, and the remains of sunken vessels.

INFORMATION

📍 at the base of Mount Carmel near the northern beaches of Haifa; 🚌

Jaffa (Ancient Joppa)

Israel's Old Testament seaport was Joppa. You can visit its modern location in today's Jaffa. Jaffa is hard to separate from the urban sprawl of modern Tel Aviv. Modern Jaffa is a seaside resort filled with restaurants, art galleries, and parks that host evening concerts. Behind the modern façade is one of the oldest functioning harbors in the world, although the sights, sounds, and smells of this working-class port in the first century would have been very different from those you will find in the relaxed atmosphere of the harbor today. The bobbing fishing boats offer the only hint to the way this natural harbor might have felt and appeared when it bustled with activity.

This is the area of Solomon's seaport on the Mediterranean Sea. As he planned for the substantial building projects in Jerusalem, including the temple, Solomon needed access to many board feet of quality building material that was not locally available. This kind of timber was available in the Lebanon Mountains within Phoenicia, Israel's neighbor to the north. Consequently, Solomon made arrangements with the Phoenician king, Hiram of Tyre, to harvest and float massive log rafts south on the Mediterranean Sea from Phoenicia. Once they arrived at the seaport of Joppa, workers broke down those log rafts and dragged the timber to Jerusalem (2 Chron. 2:16). Ezra made similar arrangements when he secured building materials for construction of the second temple (Ezra 3:7). The reluctant prophet Jonah used this seaport as well. He was thinking not about importing timber but about exporting himself on a ship bound for Tarshish, as far from his assigned mission station in Nineveh as he could get (Jon. 1:3). In the New Testament, Joppa witnessed a miracle performed by Peter as he raised Tabitha from the dead (Acts 9:36–43).

INFORMATION 📍 the modern port and parks are adjacent to Nemal Yafo Street; 🚫

4

Central Mountains
SOUTH

A s you travel east from the coastal plain of Israel, you will find the geography changing quickly. The gently rolling plains give way to foothills that quickly give way to the central mountains. This is a zone of some variety with changes in elevation, topography, and rainfall. But overall, you will be struck by its higher elevations and the more sharply cut profile of the rising terrain. It is these realities that made ancient travel more difficult, invasion less of a concern, and farming a real challenge for those who lived here in Bible times.

I trust that your itinerary will include numerous days in the central mountains, because it hosted more Bible history than all of the other

Mediterranean Sea

Tel Aviv

Ashdod

**WEST
BANK**

Nablus

Neot Kedumim Park

Gezer

Ashkelon

Ramallah

Judean Wilderness
(from Wadi Qelt)

Jericho

Beth
Shemesh

JERUSALEM

Bethlehem

QUMRAN NATIONAL PARK

Beit Guvrin

Elah
Valley

Dead Sea

GAZA
STRIP

Lachish

HERODIUM
NATIONAL
PARK

Hebron

En Gedi Nature Reserve

MASADA NATIONAL PARK

Arad

Beersheba
(Be'er Sheva)

JORDAN

EN AVDAT
NATIONAL
PARK

Mitzpe
Ramon

Makhtesh
Ramon

EGYPT

TIMNA
VALLEY
NATIONAL
PARK

N

0   25   50 mi
0   25   50 km

Eilat

1 Arad
2 Beersheba
3 Beth Shemesh
4 Beit Guvrin National Park
5 Dead Sea
6 Elah Valley (from Tel Azekah)
7 En Avdat National Park
8 En Gedi Nature Reserve
9 Gezer
10 Hebron (Al-Khalil)
11 Herodium (Herodion)
   National Park

12 Jericho of the New Testament
   (Tulul Abu El-Alaiq)
13 Jericho of the Old Testament
   (Tell es-Sultan)
14 Judean Wilderness
   (from Wadi Qelt)
15 Lachish
16 Makhtesh Ramon
17 Masada National Park
18 Neot Kedumim Park
19 Qumran National Park
20 Timna Valley National Park

regions combined. That is why I have broken up this zone among three chapters in this guide. This particular chapter is dedicated to the southern part of the zone and its subregions: the fertile western foothills known as the Shephelah, the dry ridges and basins of the Negev, and the even drier and more rugged Judean Wilderness.

Arad

Tel Arad National Park is located in the driest of the three Negev basins. These basins mark the southernmost reach of the promised land in Bible times. The park provides a look into how people lived in this subregion both before the time of Abraham and during the time of the kings of Judah. Its archaeology includes a unique treasure. Within the fortress at the top of the hill, Judean soldiers constructed a worship facility that duplicated many of the elements of the temple in Jerusalem. There is nothing like it in the rest of Israel.

The park consists of two areas to explore. The older is the twenty-five-acre Early Bronze city that thrived between 2850 and 2650 BC. This sprawling city went out of existence about 450 years prior to the time of Abraham, making it a good place to see that a sophisticated society was part of this land long before it became the Israelite homeland. Those first residents settled here because Arad sat at a geographical crossroads. Roads radiated from here northeast into the Dead Sea basin, north into the highlands of Judah, and southwest to Egypt. These roads carried bitumen (a tar-like substance used in the embalming process) from the Dead Sea to Egypt and Egyptian goods destined for markets in Canaan.

Four elements of this Early Bronze city stand out. First, look for the surviving segments of the eight-foot wall and tower system that defended ancient Arad. It shows just how expansive this city was. As you marvel at its size, remember that this formidable city thrived centuries before the time of Abraham. Within the wall line you will find a large pagan worship complex with its altar and libation pit (a small stone-lined hole into which liquid offerings were poured). This is infrastructure of the Canaanite worship that repeatedly challenged Israel throughout the Old Testament.

Next, walk to the reconstructed Arad House. This single-room building demonstrates the construction style common to this era, one that is distinguished from the later style of home built by the Israelites. At the lowest point of the city you will find the cistern dug to harvest and hold millions of gallons of runoff water from the slopes that tilt toward its opening. When the Israelites built the fortress on the hill above, they dug the hole deeper. They struck the water table and the cistern became a well. From this spot they carried the water uphill and filled the cistern (underground water reservoir) located within the defensive walls of the fortress. This Israelite fortress on the high ground came into being long after the Early Bronze city of Arad ceased to exist. It was an outpost that went through several design changes from 1000 to 587 BC, from the time of David until the Babylonians invaded the promised land. Despite the design changes, it always functioned in the same way. Soldiers used it to watch for the advance of Edomite soldiers who were intent on attacking Judah from the south.

The signature element of this archaeological park is the Arad sanctuary within the fort. Israelite soldiers modeled this sanctuary on the temple in Jerusalem, a place unlike the pagan temple in the Early Bronze city below. Standing in the forecourt is an altar of uncut stones (Exod. 20:25). Beyond this altar is a courtyard with incense altars, like the holy place of the temple in Jerusalem. Those incense altars stand before a small room (like the holy of holies) that contained either one or two upright stones (perhaps meant to recall two stone tablets on which Moses received the Ten Commandments). All of these parallels have produced many questions to which there are no certain answers. Was this a symbolic or functioning temple? Did it mingle pagan elements with orthodox Jewish worship? While the answers to such questions evade us, one thing is certain: this Israelite sanctuary is unique, the sole surviving Old Testament Israelite sanctuary contemporary with the first temple in Jerusalem.

Finally, from the walls of the Israelite fortress it is possible to get a sense for the Negev ecosystem in which Abraham's family lived upon entering the promised land (Gen. 12:9). The light-colored loess (wind-blown) soil of this area is rich in quartz. When the meager rainfall comes, the quartz crystals link to create a surface that sheds the life-giving moisture. Most years the grain planted here will not sustain until harvest. However, enough moisture is absorbed by the soil during the winter months to produce a flourish of spring grass favoring pastoralists like Abraham's family. As these natural pastures yield their vitality before the hot southern winds of summer, pastoralists of the Negev move their sheep and goats north in incremental steps ever deeper into the heart of Canaan where pastures linger longer. It is no wonder the Bible often describes the family of Abraham on the move, building a relationship with the promised land not with deeds but with wells, seasonal camps, and altars they built along the migration routes that led north into the land they were given on oath.

INFORMATION 📍 travel west from the modern city of Arad along Highway 80; the entry is about eight kilometers to its west; 🚗

⭐ Beersheba

Tel Beersheba National Park presents the most complete reconstruction of an Old Testament town you will meet during your trip. The name Beersheba means "well of the seven" or "well of the oath," linking it to two Bible stories set during the days of Abraham and Isaac (Gen. 21:22–34; 26:23–33).

Beersheba became a fortified city during the time of King David to discourage invasion of his kingdom from the south. The Ridge Route began here, the roadway that connected all the major cities in David's kingdom to the north of Beersheba. This route proved to be a tempting target, too tempting for the Egyptian pharaoh Shishak, who attacked and destroyed Beersheba while on his way to loot Jerusalem in 925 BC (2 Chron. 12:9). During better days that followed, Beersheba was rebuilt as an administrative center, located at an important crossroads. Merchants who picked up their trade goods in places like the Dead Sea or Arabia moved them along roads that passed through Beersheba on their way to the Mediterranean seaport of Gaza. The eighth-century town preserved for your visit collected trade revenue from these merchants.

Many dimensions of ancient Israelite culture come to life in the archaeology of this site, starting with the square stone altar in the courtyard. This is a replica of the four-horned altar discovered on this site (the original is in the Israel Museum). When archaeologists found it, the altar was not intact but broken apart and scattered throughout a variety of other ancient structures. Perhaps the religious reform of King Hezekiah or King Josiah brought its time of service to an end when altars other than those in Jerusalem were destroyed (2 Kings 18:3–4; 23:12–15). As you leave the courtyard and walk up the slope toward the town proper, you will pass two components of the town's water system. The first is a large cistern (underground water reservoir) that holds more than 132,000 gallons of water. A dam constructed across the Wadi Hebron redirects water into this reservoir during the rainy winter months. Access to the cistern is from the top of the site. The second is a 225-foot-deep well, the deepest ancient well discovered to date in Israel. Beyond the well is the fortified entry to the town. It is called a "gate" but is better thought of as a gatehouse through which an enemy soldier had to fight in order to gain access to the town proper. Note how the multichambered building is constructed with local materials. The builders used sun-dried mud brick, which rises above a fieldstone foundation. Look closely and you will see that these bricks were made with straw. This prevented them from cracking when they dried, and increased their strength as much as three times beyond bricks made without straw.

More cultural insights come to light within the town. Once inside the gate, look to the right and you will find a set of storage buildings. Merchants typically paid transit fees in a city like Beersheba by surrendering a portion of the merchandise being moved to market. These storage rooms held such products. The partially reconstructed warehouses consist of two long corridors designed for storage and a central aisle to provide access. A set of pillars on either side of this central aisle supported the roof, which included a clerestory window (an uncovered, vertical opening) that provided both ventilation and light. Finally, check out the partially reconstructed Israelite homes on the northwest side of the site. As the designation "Israelite House" suggests, this style of architecture became common in this land with the arrival of the Israelites. While there were variations, Israelite homes in this region typically consisted of a ground floor with four enclosed spaces. This floor included an open courtyard used for cooking and three perimeter rooms for storage. A second floor provided sleeping space for the family. Note that the back room of the house is built into the defensive wall of the city. This is known as the casemate room. It was available for storage during peacetime, but if the city was under attack, it could be filled with debris, effectively doubling the width of the defensive wall.

Pick a place with a view south into the Negev and consider an important decision that Jacob faced here, one intimately linked to geography (Gen. 46:1). The Lord gave Abraham a set of promises that he passed along to his family. These promises connected Abraham's family to the promised Savior from sin, and they connected the mission of this family to the land of Canaan. That is where Beersheba comes in. It is used repeatedly in the Old Testament to define the southern border of the promised land with the expression "from Dan to Beersheba" (Judg. 20:1; 1 Sam. 3:20). When Jacob arrived at this spot en route to Egypt, he hesitated. So much pulled him south toward Egypt. Joseph, the son whom he thought had died, was alive and had risen within the ranks of Egyptian government. Joseph was in control of the food distribution program in Egypt right when the region was gripped by a seven-year famine. Drawn from this land by Joseph's invitation and driven from this land by famine, Jacob had set out for Egypt. But he hesitated at Beersheba because the next steps he took would take him out of the promised land. Knowing the importance of this land to their mission and recalling the stories of his father and grandfather who had been all too quick to exit the land when famine struck in their day (Gen. 12:10–20; 26:1–6), Jacob hesitated. Only when he heard these words of assurance did Jacob leave: "I am God, the God of your father. . . . Do not be afraid to go down to Egypt, for I will make you into a great nation there. I will go down to Egypt with you, and I will surely bring you back again" (Gen. 46:3–4).

INFORMATION 📍 take Highway 60 east from modern Beersheba for five kilometers and look for the sign indicating your turn for the park entrance; 🚗

Beth Shemesh

Beth Shemesh played an important role in the return of the ark of the covenant from the Philistines at the time of Samuel, and the view from this low rise captures key moments from the life of Samson. At a mere seven acres and with little to distinguish it from its surroundings, Beth

Shemesh does not look like much. But it had real strategic value for those living in Bible times. Canaanites, Philistines, and Israelites all took their turn building a town here.

As you walk up into the site, the Sorek Valley will come into view. This is an ideal place to develop your understanding of the Judean Shephelah, the foothills that separate the higher mountains and the coastal plain. These foothills provided the setting for many Bible stories. No matter where you travel in this subregion, its geographical architecture looks the same. The Shephelah consists of wide U-shaped valleys confined between lower east–west ridges. It is the latter that gives the Shephelah its name. In Hebrew, Shephelah means "humble." These humble hills and their associated valleys had much to offer. In Bible times the hillsides were filled with sycamore trees whose limbs were cut and used as roof rafters (1 Kings 10:27). The wide valleys produced a wonderful grain harvest fed by the high-nutrient soil that washed into them from the mountains to the east. And for those on the move, these east–west valleys formed natural travel corridors from the coastal plain to the interior of Judah.

This archaeological site is less developed for your visit, so you will find a number of ancient ruins but no help in determining what they are. The most prominent archaeological feature on the site is a Byzantine religious complex found on the southeast side. But it is the northeast side where archaeologists continue to uncover Beth Shemesh of the Old Testament era. Look for a room with three large, flat stones all in a line. Scholars have concluded that this was a pagan temple with altar stones dating to the eleventh century BC, the time of Samuel. The evidence indicates that those who destroyed this temple sought to desecrate it, and so disable its deities, by using its location as an animal pen. Other structures on this side of the site were part of an Israelite administrative center dating to the tenth century BC. Among its buildings, you can explore an underground, cross-shaped cistern that could store over 211,000 gallons of water.

Bible readers can think about two Old Testament episodes here. Much of Samson's troubling story and his repeated conflicts with the Philistines occurred within sight of Beth Shemesh. His hometown was Zorah, located on the ridge just to your north. The story of his proposed marriage in Timnah, a lion attack, grain fields set on fire, and his betrayal by Delilah all find their place in the valley before you (Judg. 13–16).

A story that directly engages Beth Shemesh is found in 1 Samuel 6:1–7:1. Here the inspired author mentions the city repeatedly in order to demonstrate the fading spiritual health of Israel. To get the larger picture, you need to begin by reading this story in 1 Samuel 4. The Israelites took the ark of the covenant into battle; the Philistines defeated them and captured the ark. The Philistines moved it from one city to the next, only to have it cause trouble wherever it went. When the ark arrived at Ekron, a Philistine city located on the west side of the Sorek Valley, the Philistine leaders looked for a way to return it to Israel without bringing more harm to their own citizens. They did so by hitching cows that had recently calved to a cart containing the ark, which they sent down the Sorek Valley toward Beth Shemesh. Everything seemed to go fine until the residents of Beth Shemesh looked into the ark and were struck dead. As the writer tells the story, Beth Shemesh is mentioned nine times in just eleven verses. To understand this repetition, we need to see that Beth Shemesh played a special role in Israelite culture. It was one of the Levitical cities where Israel's clergy lived (Josh. 21:16). Think of the implications for the story about the ark's return. If there was a town that should have known how to manage themselves around the ark, this was it. Their failure helps communicate to the readers of 1 Samuel just how low the spiritual health of Israel had sunk.

INFORMATION 📍 on the west side of Highway 38 near modern Beth Shemesh; 🚫

Beit Guvrin National Park

Beit Guvrin National Park is a 1,250-acre park that preserves the Old Testament city of Maresha (Greek Marisa) and the nearby Roman city of Beit Guvrin. Here you have a chance to connect with Rehoboam, Solomon's son. He fortified this site as part of the larger plan to deter invasion of Judah by the most travel-friendly routes. This is also a place to learn more about the geology and natural history of this region. The stop associated with the Bell Caves will give you that opportunity.

Layers of Old Testament history lie beneath your feet as you walk this park. Rehoboam fortified Maresha (2 Chron. 11:5–11). Invading Assyrians destroyed the place in the eighth century BC (Mic. 1:15). And following the deportation of Jews by Babylon (sixth century BC), it was claimed by the invading Edomites, who became known as the Idumeans. They made this city their regional capital. From this point on, the city became a cultural melting pot that included Jewish, Egyptian, Sidonian, and Greek elements. Ironically, the tell (archaeological mound) offers little more than an elevated view of the area because of a unique demand the Ottomans placed on the archaeologists who excavated here. The Ottomans required the archaeologists to leave the site as they found it. That meant all the streets and structures uncovered during the archaeological investigation had to be backfilled, and so they remain out of sight below your feet.

If you are interested in geology and natural history, stop at the Bell Caves parking area. Here a short natural history walk will introduce you to the local trees and plants as you weave through a series of manmade caves. These caves were created in the sixth to tenth century AD by those in pursuit of the soft chalk that was used to make mortar and plaster. The miners opened a series of one-meter holes that you will see at the top of the caves, excavating down to create the bell shape that gives these caves their name. A walk in them offers a view of the beautiful geologic architecture that lies unseen beneath our feet in the Shephelah.

If you are interested in ancient culture, other underground sections of this park await your visit. Well-marked trails lead to a massive cross-shaped columbarium (arti-

INFORMATION
 along Highway 35 southwest of Jerusalem;

ficial nesting area created to attract doves), a reconstructed olive oil processing factory, and the ornately painted Sidonian tombs (third to second century BC).

⭐ Dead Sea

There are few places on earth so beautiful and so forbidding as the Dead Sea. When you stand on its shore, you are standing at the lowest point on the surface of the earth—1,300 feet below sea level. And when you touch its water, you are experiencing one of the most chemically laden lakes on earth, with salt content approaching 33 percent (nearly nine times that of the ocean).

The Dead Sea fills just the top of the spectacular geologic rift created when two tectonic plates, the African and Arabian, parted company. While the deepest part of the Dead Sea is over one thousand feet, it is estimated that unconsolidated bedrock below this body of water lies another twenty thousand feet down, making this the deepest tear in the surface of the earth. Water arrives in the basin primarily via the Jordan River. But upriver demands have curtailed inbound flow to less than 5 percent of what it was in Bible times, resulting in a rapidly dropping lake level and the formation of sinkholes that you will see adjacent to the road. There is no natural outlet for the water that enters, so the only way for the water to leave is through evaporation. There is plenty of that, particularly on a summer day when daytime high temperatures exceed 100°F. On such a day, half an inch of water leaves the lake, creating the perpetual haze that fills the Dead Sea basin. The beautiful blue-green color of the water looks so inviting on a hot summer day. But few who visit the lakeside beaches call the water refreshing. They come for the therapeutic value of the water and cosmetic value of the mud. And who can refuse "swimming" in a body of water that does not allow you to sink? Just be cautious about ingesting water or getting it in your eyes or into a cut. The salt will add unforgettable discomfort to the unforgettable view.

INFORMATION

📍 along Highway 90 south of Jericho; 🚫

The Bible mentions this body of water under a variety of names, including Salt Sea, Eastern Sea, and Sea of the Arabah. The most striking mention of the Dead Sea occurs in Ezekiel 47:8–12, where its change is used to illustrate the dramatic refashioning of the world that the Messiah will bring at the end of time. In this vision, Ezekiel sees a deepening water stream flowing from the temple in Jerusalem. It flows into the Dead Sea and completely changes the ecosystem. The lifeless inland lake without fruit trees or fishermen becomes a life-filled inland lake.

⭐ Elah Valley (from Tel Azekah)

The story of David's battle with Goliath is one of the best-known stories in the Bible. But the geography that begins and ends the story (1 Sam. 17:1–4, 51–53) often goes unappreciated. That can change for you when you put this story on the land at Tel Azekah. From here you will have a commanding view of the Elah Valley and the unfamiliar geography that introduces this familiar story.

As you make your climb to the top of the hill, catch the views west. You are looking toward the coastal plain and the Mediterranean Sea. This was the region controlled by the Philistines. Look carefully for what appears to be a small hill rising about five and a half miles to the west. This is Old Testament Gath (Tell es-Safi), hometown of Goliath.

Now walk to the east side of Tel Azekah for the view down the Elah Valley toward the central mountains of Judah. This beautiful valley is part of the Shephelah (see the description under Beth Shemesh). In Saul's day it had several vital contributions to make to his young kingdom. This valley offered ready-made grain fields, timber covered hillsides, and easy access between Judah's hill country and the coast. Add all of these up and you have one of the most valuable pieces of real estate in the promised land.

As the story of David and Goliath unfolds in 1 Samuel 17, the first four verses are full of geographical details that can be traced in the view ahead of you. The Philistines have left the coastal plain and now fill the Elah Valley between where you are standing at Azekah and Socoh. Socoh is located well east of your position. With your eyes, follow the road in the valley below until you come to the place where the valley narrows near a water reservoir. To the south of the reservoir is a small hill. That is Socoh. The Philistine camp extended from where you are standing to Socoh, which means the only portion of the Elah Valley left for Saul and the Israelite soldiers was the tiny corner at the base of the mountains.

The author of 1 Samuel paints this picture with geographical references in order to help us understand the national crisis that lies behind the familiar story. The Philistines had captured a vitally important valley. What is more, they were poised to take the far eastern side of it at the base of the mountains. If they were successful in getting past Saul and the Israelite army, they would have access to a variety of routes that led from the eastern end of this valley into the mountains and to the critical Ridge Route. Access to this main road through Judah's interior would mean the Philistines could conduct raids on all the cities and villages along the north–south spine of the mountains, including Bethlehem. The geography that begins the story is not trivia. It is vital to our appreciation of the national crisis that was unfolding in this valley and the inconsequential contribution of the current king of Israel. Saul had failed to inspire faith or courage in his soldiers, and he had failed to deliver a plan of action to prevent this slow-moving disaster from unfolding further.

It was only when David arrived that everything changed. David spoke words of faith. He formulated a wise plan of action and courageously executed it. As Goliath lay dying in the valley near Socoh, the Israelite soldiers saw in David a leader they could follow. This cowering band became infused with courage and took off in hot pursuit of the Philistines. And as the story closes, the geographical picture could not be more different from the one that begins it. The Elah Valley, once full of enemy soldiers, has been purged of all but dead Philistines, with the few survivors fleeing west in the direction of the coastal plain (1 Sam. 17:51–53). This is the geographical turn of events that points to David rather than Saul as the best man to lead Israel as king.

INFORMATION 📍 in the British Park accessed by taking Highway 38 south of Beth Shemesh and driving to the park entrance located off Route 383 west; drive to the highest elevation in the park and look for the parking area and signs directing you to the top of Tel Azekah, a fifteen-minute walk away; 🚫

En Avdat National Park

To experience all the beauty and austerity of the southern wilderness, travel to En Avdat National Park. The Lord kept Israel in this region for thirty-eight years. Only after using the geography of this region to humble, test, and teach them (Deut. 8:1–3) did he bring Israel into the promised land.

Driving the roads in the park will give you a taste of the southern wilderness, but there is no better way to experience wilderness than with a walk starting at the lower parking lot. You have two options.

The first will take about an hour. It is an out-and-back hike through the canyon to a waterfall and its accompanying pool. The natural beauty of this walk will take your breath away. Wind and water have sculpted the soft limestone walls of this canyon into a bizarre limestone mural that is laced with black seams of flint. Although the area receives only four to eight inches of annual precipitation, rainfall drains into this canyon from a large watershed, forming its waterfall and stream. This water gives birth to the array of shrubs, trees, and wildlife you will see in this nature reserve. The second hiking option is a one-way walk that follows the same trail to the waterfalls but then climbs out of the canyon on stairs and ladders en route to the upper parking lot. This hike will take two to three hours and requires that you work out a transportation plan since you will be finishing in a different location than where you began.

The Lord brought Israel into the wilderness after their stay in Egypt in order to humble them, to test them, and to teach them that he was worthy of their trust (Deut. 8:1–3). After two years in the wilderness, he looked for signs of that faith as he invited them to enter the promised land. Unthinkably, Israel refused the invitation. As a result, all the adults responsible for this decision faced death in the wilderness where Israel would remain for an additional thirty-eight years (Num. 14:20–35). Certainly everyone would have died quickly were it not for the repeated miracles the Lord provided, producing food and water in a place that had neither in sufficient quantity to preserve the lives of hundreds, much less tens of thousands. It was during one of those miracles that Moses and Aaron failed to model the trust that the wilderness was to build. As a result, the Lord barred both from entering the promised land (Num. 20:1–12). But the wilderness continued to perform its role for the next generation of Israel, humbling them, testing their faith, and teaching them. By walking in this wilderness, you can

> **INFORMATION**
> 📍 on High-
> way 40 south of
> Beersheba; 🚻

acquire a sense of how this ecosystem participated in Israel's development as the people of God, just as our own "wilderness" seasons of
life have a role in shaping us as God's own.

⭐ En Gedi Nature Reserve

David hid in the En Gedi area as the murderous Saul relentlessly pursued him. But here he faced another threat: death by dehydration.
That is why he spent a portion of his wilderness time near this oasis
now secured within the En Gedi Nature Reserve. At the oasis, the
bland yellows and treeless ridges of the Judean Wilderness give way to
refreshing blue water and green foliage. This 250-acre park preserves
the natural world of a wilderness oasis so that visitors can appreciate
the uniqueness of this ecosystem and the role it played in David's life.

Hiking trails of varying length and difficulty provide access to this
wonder-filled world. We will focus on the loop that meanders through
the lower falls, up to David's Waterfall, and circles back to the parking
lot. It takes one and a half hours and is of moderate difficulty because
of the climbing involved. A shorter and less rigorous out-and-back
segment leads to the lower falls.

Where does the water come from? This is the first question you
are likely to ask in this rain-deprived region. The water that flows here
and in all the other oases in the Judean Wilderness fell as rain on the
western slopes of Judah's mountains. Over thousands of years, these
persistent rains eroded the limestone and moved the surface watershed
line of Judah's mountains to the east. This changed the way water flowed
on the surface but not underground where the subsurface watershed
line remained in its original location farther to the west. This means
that a portion of rain that falls on the western slopes of Judah's mountains travels underground in the direction of the Dead Sea (rather
than toward the Mediterranean Sea) and breaks out as springs and
streams in the wilderness. This water produces the thriving natural

world protected in this reserve. It is a living classroom in which you can meet oasis plants like ferns, bamboo-like reeds, date palm, acacia, Egyptian balsam, and Christ thorn. It is also the place to see and learn about birds and animals like Tristram's starlings, the desert tawny owl, the Nubian ibex (the wild goat for which the park is named), the rock hyrax, and the fennec fox.

This wilderness and oasis play an important role in David's story. As a young man, David experienced a meteoric rise in popularity following his defeat of Goliath. But it was just this popularity that inspired the sitting king, Saul, to relentlessly pursue him with the intention of ending his life. David retreated to the wilderness, acquiring food on the fringes and water from oases within, including the oasis at En Gedi (1 Sam. 24:1). David achieved a measure of security here in this ecosystem so hostile to human habitation. And in turn, the Lord used the wilderness to mature David's faith. The austere wilderness and dire personal circumstances of David humbled him, taught him to respect his own limitations, and grew his trust in the Lord.

On one occasion, this wilderness provided David with a chance to reveal his growing faith. David and his men were hiding from Saul in a cave in the En Gedi area when Saul entered that same cave to use it as a bathroom. Despite the opportune moment and the encouragement of his men, David did not dispatch his rival. Instead, he trusted the Lord to work out the transition to the throne in his own time. David spared Saul's life, and in doing so, he showed just how much his trust in the Lord had grown (1 Sam. 24:1–22). Finally, the wilderness made one more contribution to the life of David that we enjoy as a legacy of his time here. This place that developed his perspective on life also gave David imagery when writing poetic verse. Find a quiet spot in the reserve to read Psalms 57 and 63. The language of these psalms reveals their wilderness heritage.

INFORMATION
📍 on High-
way 90 south of
Qumran; 🔄

Gezer

The size of an archaeological site and a long history of repeated use through the centuries are signs of importance. Tel Gezer has both. Its ruins cover some thirty-three acres. The site remained in use from the seventeenth century BC to the Hellenistic period. That means people lived here from the time Israel was in Egypt to the close of the Old Testament. Its residents left behind three very unique treasures to explore: a gate from the time of Solomon, an underground water system, and a set of ten large standing stones.

To get oriented, walk to the raised lookout platform on the west side of the site. From here you will be able to appreciate the importance of Gezer's geographical setting. To the west is the Mediterranean Sea and the coastal plain. The International Highway that connected the markets of Asia, Africa, and Europe traveled on this plain just west of Gezer. To the east you will see the broad Aijalon Valley. The Jericho–Gezer road traveled through this valley, ascending the Beth Horon Ridge to your east en route to Jerusalem. This was the route that connected Jerusalem with the world's markets and invading armies with Jerusalem.

That is what made Gezer such an amazing wedding gift, an importance underscored by its threefold mention in 1 Kings 9:15–17. The Egyptian pharaoh, Siamum, was involved in a dispute with the Canaanites. To acquire the support of Solomon, he gave one of his daughters to Solomon as a bride, defeated the Canaanites living in Gezer, and then gave this city to Solomon as a wedding present (1 Kings 9:16). As you might expect, Solomon quickly fortified this key city (1 Kings 9:15, 17). The foundation of a six-chambered gate and accompanying wall lines located on the south side of the site may well be part of that fortification process.

You can explore the even earlier water system located on the southwest side of the site. This water system dates to the Late Bronze era.

That means it served a city associated with the Canaanites who lived here during the days of Joshua and Judges (Josh. 10:33; 16:10; Judg. 1:29). It provided secure access to water via a tunnel and pool. Like many archaeological treasures in Israel, a fuller understanding of its architecture and how it functioned is still under investigation.

On the north side of the archaeological site are ten large, upright stones and an accompanying water basin. Someone intentionally put these standing stones in this location during the Middle Bronze period. But while we know they were set up during the time of Abraham's family, their significance and role are debated. They could represent ten deities whose spirit resided in them. That would make this a worship site to which people came in order to interact with these deities. On the other hand, these ten stones could represent ten satellite villages that had made a treaty with Gezer. The installation was then a symbol of that agreement.

Gezer itself is not mentioned frequently in the Bible, but it is a good place to think about why God may have chosen this land as his promised land. Two goals were accomplished in his selection of this land. First, the Lord needed to create a secure location for Israel, one that would allow them to live in isolation from empire armies and the paganism of the larger world. The mountains to the east provided that security and isolation. At the same time, the Lord needed to create access for the message of salvation linked to his chosen people. That access was available just west of the mountains via the International Highway that traversed the coastal plain. From Gezer, poised between mountains and the coastal plain, we can see that the promised land is uniquely positioned to accomplish both goals.

INFORMATION 📍 turn east off Highway 44 into Karmi Yoseph; follow Tamar Street to Gefen Street, which will lead to Tel Gezer, located north of Karmi Yoseph; 🚫

Hebron (Al-Khalil)

Abraham's family tomb is in Hebron. That makes it a city of great spiritual importance to Jews, Christians, and Muslims, because all three of these religions honor Abraham's role in their faith tradition. This city was also the first capital city of King David following the death of Saul and remained David's capital during the seven-and-a-half-year civil war that followed (2 Sam. 5:1–5).

When Sarah, Abraham's wife, died, it became necessary for him to purchase land for his family's tomb. Although Canaan was the promised land, the deedless Abraham regarded himself as an alien and stranger who had to bargain with the locals for a plot of ground and its cave that he might use for a family tomb (Gen. 23). Once the land was purchased, Abraham buried Sarah here. In the years that followed, Abraham, Isaac, Jacob, and their wives would join her. In the first century BC, Herod the Great built an ornate wall encircling the parcel of land presumed to be the land Abraham purchased. It was called the Machpelah (Cave of the Patriarchs).

The building is part mosque and part synagogue, so you will need to pick one of the two entrances for your visit. Within the building you will see six cenotaphs. These are not coffins but memorial structures that reside above the cave in which the burials took place. The cenotaphs of Abraham and Sarah are in the middle of the building, with Sarah's cenotaph positioned north of Abraham's. The cenotaphs of Jacob and Leah are on the west side, with Leah's cenotaph to the north of Jacob's. The cenotaphs of Isaac and Rebekah lie on the east side; Rebekah's cenotaph is north of Isaac's. Access to the cave below is not permitted.

Abraham purchased this parcel of land not only to serve as the family tomb but also as a memorial for his descendants, a place to reflect on the critical link between Abraham's family and their assigned mission. God promised Abraham that his family would become a thriving nation. God promised Abraham that his family-turned-nation would have Canaan as their homeland. And God promised that from that nation on this land he would provide the blessing of forgiveness to the nations (Gen. 12:1–3). Because this was the first parcel of land to be truly owned by Abraham's family, it was special. It was the first step in the fulfillment of the land promise. What is more, its location on the main road traveling north and south through the heart of Canaan meant Abraham's descendants could visit this tomb repeatedly as they traveled on the Ridge Route. In the end it became and still is what he intended it to be: a place to recall and reflect on the powerful promises that linked this family and this land.

One more insight is to be gained here, one that is related to how the temple in Jerusalem would have looked. Notice the way the exterior walls are constructed with meticulously trimmed ashlars (large, square building stones), each laid without the use of mortar. Here you can also see pilasters (engaged columns), which give the building a sense of strength and height. Herod the Great, who built this structure, also expanded the temple complex in Jerusalem. We are unable to see the temple complex in Jerusalem because the Romans destroyed it in AD 70. But here we can get a sense for its design features in a building of Herod that the Romans did not destroy.

INFORMATION 📍 Hebron is thirty kilometeres south of Jerusalem on Highway 60; once in Hebron, watch for the signs that lead to the Cave of the Patriarchs; 🚫 🏛

⭐ Herodium (Herodion) National Park

The Herodium is a spectacular palace built by Herod the Great. It was part safe house to which he could flee, part lookout station against invaders from the east, part luxury palace for the entertainment of his guests, and part monumental tomb designed to be his final resting place. It was also a place Jesus used to illustrate a lesson more spectacular in content than Herod's palace, a lesson on the power of prayer.

Begin your visit with a walk up the steep ramp to the rim of the upper palace. As you start your climb, look down and to your left. That is where you will find the sprawling and luxurious lower palace of the Herodium. Its most distinguishing feature is the swimming pool with its signature island in the middle. Herod surrounded this pool with a formal garden and buildings filled with luxurious amenities and art, the perfect place for Herod's guests to relax.

Continue climbing and walk to the northeast side of the rim. From there the geographical context of the Herodium and its role as a lookout station will become clear. To the west you will see Judah's hill country. Bethlehem is in view to the northwest, and the towers on the Mount of Olives to the north mark the location of Jerusalem. To the east lies the Judean Wilderness, the Dead Sea, and the even higher mountains of modern Jordan. It is particularly this view to the east that made the Herodium a valuable lookout station. Invaders from the Transjordan had to begin their trip across the Judean Wilderness where they could stock up on water, at a place like En Gedi located along the shoreline of the Dead Sea. An ancient road went from En Gedi, above the deeply cut Wadi Tekoa that lies to your south, on its way to Judah's interior. No invader could make this trek without passing within view of the Herodium, making it a key eastern lookout station.

As you look down into the circular interior of Herod's upper palace, you get a sense of the engineering feat required to make this place possible. First, the interior of the hill you are standing on was hollowed out. Then Herod built a five-story, circular building at the base of and around the perimeter of this excavated recess. The most distinguishing features of this building were its four towers, whose bases are still intact. As you can see, the round tower on the east side of the complex was the largest. It was mostly solid and would have extended an additional eighty feet above its current foundation. Three other semicircular towers are found on the north, west, and south sides of the complex. These were hollow and contained storage and living space. Once Herod had the circular halls and towers in place, he shaved the soil and rock from the adjacent hill (just north of the current complex) and moved it to the Herodium building site in order to create the steep exterior slopes that covered two stories of the previously built halls. This added to the grandeur of its appearance while enhancing its security.

With your impressions collected, descend via the modern staircase for a look at the hollowed-out interior. A walk through the remains of the upper palace, although stripped of its fine fabrics and exotic decorations, will give you a taste for its extravagance. You can visit the remains of Herod's dining room, his Roman hot bath, and his peristyle garden. All were designed for his personal pleasure and the enjoyment of his guests.

The utilitarian portions of the palace can be seen by going underground. Look for a set of stairs located just below the large eastern tower base. As you descend, you will walk past cisterns built to hold the water that served the complex. The three largest cisterns held approximately 660,430 gallons of water. During the Second Jewish Revolt against Rome (AD 132–35), the Jewish resistors seized control of this location and turned it into an administrative center. The synagogue and ritual baths you saw above and part of the tunnel system you are walking through are part of their legacy at the Herodium.

Once you are outside, there is one more important area to visit. It houses the private theater of Herod and the remains of his tomb. For a long time, the ancient reports of Herod's burial at the Herodium were questioned because no monumental tomb had been found. That changed in 2007 when Ehud Netzer discovered evidence of a lavish burial and the foundation of a multistory mausoleum that was as large as seven stories tall. Its massive base is all that survives and lies beyond the remains of the private theater.

Here at the tomb with Bethlehem on the horizon to the west, you can reflect on the striking difference between the Roman-appointed king of Judea and Jesus, the divinely appointed King of the Jews. Jesus was born in Herod's last days, when his mental state had deteriorated. This once-great leader and builder was now filled with paranoia. He ordered the execution of family members whom he feared to be conspiring against him. When the magi came looking for the King of the Jews, they touched off another bout of paranoia. Herod gave orders to kill the baby boys in the village of Bethlehem, perhaps sending soldiers from this very facility to accomplish the grisly task (Matt. 2:1–12).

Although the Herodium is not mentioned by name in the Bible, it is the distinctive mountain Jesus had in view from the Mount of Olives when he spoke with the disciples about the power of prayer (Matt. 21:18–22). The Herodium was a symbol of all that had gone so horribly wrong in Israel. It symbolized misuse of power and the misuse of wealth. It was the epitome of social injustice and misplaced values. The disciples felt powerless in the face of such challenges. What could they do when Herod could do this? Jesus answered, "Pray." Herod may have been able to move a mountain, but so could they. "If you have faith and do not doubt, . . . you can say to this mountain, 'Go, throw yourself into the sea,' and it will be done. If you believe, you will receive whatever you ask for in prayer" (Matt. 21:21–22).

INFORMATION 📍 take Highway 60 south from Jerusalem and then Route 398 to the park entrance; 🌐

Jericho of the New Testament (Tulul Abu El-Alaiq)

Jesus's ministry reached into the lives of both the impoverished and the wealthy. That may best be illustrated in Jericho. Here two men, who lived in the same city but under very different circumstances, changed because they met Jesus. Their names are Bartimaeus and Zacchaeus.

This archaeological site makes you work a bit more to appreciate its wonders because it is poorly developed and interpreted for the visitor. The most striking structures are those built by Herod the Great. He was taking advantage of the geography here. Although a mere fifteen miles from Jerusalem, this oasis in the Judean Wilderness was a very different place. It offered water, agricultural products, and temperatures 30°F warmer than Jerusalem. The warmer temperatures made Jericho a winter resort for the rich and famous, including Herod the Great. The mud-brick superstructures of his palaces have long since worn away, leaving only foundations of his once great buildings. Herod's last palace in Jericho (and the one in which he died) straddled the wadi (the often-dry riverbed). Start your visit on the south side with the view from the top of the mound. This mound likely housed a round hall used for relaxing and dining. To its east you will see a large swimming pool, and to the west was a lavish sunken garden. The bridge that crossed the wadi is now gone, so you will have to cross the streambed to reach the north side of the complex. Here you can wander through the remains of a reception hall, multiple courtyards, and a Roman bathhouse. In this area you will find evidence of the signature construction techniques Herod used in his buildings. On the floor of the palace, you can make out patterned indentations that contained tiles (*opus sectile*). And where the brickwork of the walls survives, you will see that the bricks have been set on edge in a diamond pattern (*opus reticulatum*). Both styles betray a European heritage so loved by Herod.

Bartimaeus and Zacchaeus both lived in Jericho but in very different parts of its social world. Bartimaeus was poor. Although he was unable to see the wealthy estates around him, blind Bartimaeus knew they were there. He begged from those who passed by to make ends meet. That is how he spent his days until he met Jesus at the edge of the city. Bartimaeus called out, "Son of David, have mercy on me!" Jesus did, and this impoverished man received his sight (Mark 10:46–52). The second Jericho story (Luke 19:1–9) takes us to the opposite side of the economic spectrum. Here we meet Zacchaeus, a tax collector who had done quite well for himself. He too faced a physical limitation, but one far less serious than that of Bartimaeus. When Jesus comes by, Zacchaeus does not call out. But being short of stature, he climbs a sycamore tree to see Jesus. His spiritual needs were the same as those of Bartimaeus. Jesus saw these needs and invited himself to dinner at this tax collector's home to bring salvation to his household. Both stories are Jericho stories. In them we meet two men with different limitations from different sides of the social world of Jericho, but with the same need, a need filled by Jesus, the only Savior.

> **INFORMATION** 📍 follow the signs in modern Jericho; these will lead you to the south side of the city where the Wadi Qelt drains into the Jordan Valley; 🚫

⭐ Jericho of the Old Testament (Tell es-Sultan)

The story of Jericho and its tumbling walls (Josh. 6) is among the best known in the Bible. But long before Joshua and the Israelites attacked it, others found Jericho too important to pass up. It is the oldest town in the world (8000 BC) as well as the lowest in elevation (825 feet below sea level).

You will be able to see the geographical advantages of Jericho better than its ancient walls and buildings that eroded away long ago. The Elisha Spring, located just east of the ruin (2 Kings 2:19–22), gushes at a rate of 1,200 gallons per minute, turning the barren wilderness into an agriculturally productive oasis filled with date palms. The trees' presence signals the existence of subterranean water that feeds the extensive groves. These give the city its other name—the City of Palms

(Deut. 34:3). A consistent water supply joined with agriculture to attract the first settlers to Jericho, who defended their village by constructing a large defensive tower. You can see the round tower with its internal set of stairs at the bottom of a pit on the west side of the excavation. As you look down, you are looking back in time to

Old Testament cities were defended by multiple layers of protection designed to delay attackers, cause casualties, and plant seeds of discouragement.

1 Entry ramp
2 Revetment wall
3 Glacis
4 Main defensive wall
5 Gatehouse

the eighth millennium BC, when ground level was at the bottom of this pit. To put it in perspective, people were living here five thousand years before Abraham.

Many Bible readers come to Jericho expecting to see walls from the time of Joshua. They are gone, the victims of human destruction and natural erosion. Nevertheless, here and there you will glimpse earlier walls dating to the Early and Middle Bronze eras (periods that overlap with the stories we read in Genesis and Exodus). Although the walls do not date to the time of Joshua, it is important to look carefully at them. These are walls made of sun-dried mud bricks, the same kind of wall that fell before Joshua.

On the south side of the excavation, you will get the best picture of how Canaanite cities of Joshua's day defended themselves. Not just one defensive wall but layers of protection were designed to delay the advance of enemy soldiers and to multiply casualties among those who pressed the attack. The outermost wall of the two that encircled Jericho was located where you see the massive curving wall of field-stone. This was the foundation for the outer defensive wall of the city, which doubled as a retaining wall (known as a revetment wall). Above this fieldstone foundation (which was mostly underground), imagine a mud-brick superstructure. This lower wall presented an imposing barrier but, once breached, did not put the attackers in the city. Just inside this outer revetment wall, the attacker faced a steep, exposed slope called a glacis. This slope offered no cover from the arrows fired from above by the city's defenders. And if an attacking solider was able to cross this exposed zone, he was still not in the city but only at the base of Jericho's inner defensive wall. This picture of Jericho's defensive system helps us appreciate just how many Israelite lives were spared when the Lord caused the wall of Jericho to collapse, allowing everyone to charge straight in (Josh. 6:20).

As impressive as these defenses are, most Bible readers imagine seeing a larger fort than they find here. Jericho was no more than ten acres in size. Why didn't the Israelites just go around it? The impor-tance of Jericho was defined not by its size but by its strategic location. A natural route descended from the ridges above Jericho to the east where the King's Highway traveled the watershed of the Transjordan mountains. This route crossed the natural ford of the Jordan River before continuing to Jericho, where water could be obtained for the next leg of the journey. With their water replenished, the ancient merchants or soldiers could make the eight- to ten-hour crossing of the Judean Wilderness using the natural routes leading through the wilderness to the mountain interior of Judah. Here travelers or invaders could access the Ridge Route, which provided access to every major town or city of the interior. Alternately merchants or travelers could continue past the Ridge Route to the coastal plain and connect with the International Highway. Thus the east–west route, which we call the Jericho–Gezer Road, cut completely through the promised land, connecting international roadways that traveled the Transjordan mountains to your east and the coastal plain out of sight to your west. Jericho is the geographical bottleneck along this route and so the ideal place to control movement and collect tariffs. If Joshua had left this fort intact, it would have been a continuing problem, particularly since many Israelites had families they had left on the east side of the Jordan River. That is why the Lord brought it down. And once he did so, Joshua proposed the unthinkable: leave it in ruin (Josh. 6:26). This was a call to faith. The Lord promised his protection and blessing to the Israelites, urging them to move forward to other Canaanite forts rather than refortify this critical city. This appears to be a policy that Israel kept until the unfortunate time of King Ahab, when Jericho was rebuilt (1 Kings 16:34).

> **INFORMATION** 📍 follow the signs in the modern city of Jericho for Tell es-Sultan, located in its northwestern quarter; 🚻

✪ Judean Wilderness (from Wadi Qelt)

The Judean Wilderness is an austere and forbidding region, one of the last places you might think of visiting. Yet it was the setting for a number of well-known Bible stories, including the work of John the Baptist (Matt. 3:1; Luke 1:80), the temptation of Jesus (Matt. 4:1–4), and the parable of the good Samaritan (Luke 10:25–37). To really get a sense of the wilderness, it is necessary to find a place in this region where you can find isolation from others. The parking area above the Wadi Qelt is just such a place. Be sure to bring water and walk only as far as you are comfortable when exploring.

The Judean Wilderness is approximately ten miles wide and sixty miles long, extending north and south along the western shore of the Dead Sea. In most places it looks like the view in front of you, a series of east–west ridges that plunge dramatically into narrow twisting canyons. The natural beauty of the landscape is offset by its lack of water. This region resides within a rainfall shadow. Moist air masses driven eastward from the Mediterranean Sea are forced to climb the central mountains to your west. As the air rises, it cools, producing clouds and rainfall west of the central watershed. However, when those same air masses cross the watershed, they begin to descend and warm. This causes the rainfall to stop and the clouds to evaporate, leaving a rainfall shadow that is apparent in the view and in the rainfall data. Although they are a mere fifteen miles apart, Jerusalem receives twenty-two inches of annual precipitation while Jericho receives just five inches.

How was this wilderness used? People in Bible times grew grain everywhere they could. The wilderness was not such a place. Inadequate rainfall, steep slopes, and marginal soil made agriculture impossible here. During the season of the winter rains, isolated pastures develop that are still used by the local shepherds to graze their flocks in this stingy landscape. Apart from shepherds, the wilderness was home to those who wanted to get away from others in society. In Bible times, the list included robbers, revolutionaries, and ascetics.

The wilderness is one of the best ecosystems for mortals to reflect on their own limitations and to advance their trust in the Lord. By design, a wilderness experience can humble, test, and teach (Deut. 8:2–3). Jesus entered this wilderness as Israel had entered a wilderness centuries before (Matt. 4:1–4). Both Israel and Jesus faced the same challenging question directed to them by the heavenly Father:

"Will you trust me even when the fundamentals for survival are not in view?" But the outcome could not have been more different. Israel complained about the lack of food and demanded that they be taken from the wilderness. Jesus stayed in the wilderness, chose to remain hungry, and replied to Satan's temptation by quoting the very words used to define the purpose of a wilderness experience: it is a place to learn that "man does not live on bread alone but on every word that comes from the mouth of the LORD" (Deut. 8:3; Matt. 4:4). In doing so, Jesus not only provided the obedience Israel had failed to deliver in the wilderness; he also modeled how to respond when his followers face seasons of wilderness in their lives.

David also spent time in this wilderness. During the winter months when grain was growing in the village farm fields, the shepherds had to take their sheep and goats to another location. That was when herdsmen like David moved their livestock to the wilderness pastures. Here David observed the way in which the members of his flock trusted him. He longed to trust the Lord in the same way. David's thoughts turned into words, and the Holy Spirit provided the church with one of the great treasures of the Bible, Psalm 23. This piece of poetry that so beautifully portrays the theme of trust in the Lord is best read and understood against the backdrop of the wilderness pasture that provided David with the images that make it come to life.

> **INFORMATION** 📍 take Highway 1 east from Jerusalem toward Jericho and watch for the sign for Wadi Qelt; exit north and look for a pullout with unmarked trails; 🚫

Lachish

Lachish may not be a name you recognize, but in the minds of the biblical authors, Lachish was second in military importance only to

Jerusalem. Fortified initially by King Rehoboam (2 Chron. 11:5–10), Lachish grew to become massive in scale. Its purpose was to guard the road systems that led from the southern coastal plain through Judah's interior to Jerusalem.

Three archaeological installations will help you understand the story of Lachish. Just a few steps from the parking area and to your right as you face the site you will encounter what remains of the siege ramp built by the Assyrians during their assault of Lachish in 701 BC. Their goal was to reach the city walls above with their siege equipment, devices meant to pick away at the defensive wall of the city. To build the siege ramp, the Assyrians hauled in nineteen thousand tons of rubble. Their attack was wisely directed next to, rather than at, the main gate of the city. The gate was closed during the Assyrian assault, but it is open for you. Walk up the ramp ahead of you and note the size of this gate's architectural footprint. If its ruins still impress, imagine how the intact entry must have looked with its outer courtyard and inner gatehouse. From the gate area, walk to the west-central part of the city to visit the foundation of a citadel measuring 115 feet by 250 feet, the largest pre-Roman citadel discovered to date in Israel. It held multiple buildings and offered a commanding view of the area.

Biblical scholars and historians of the ancient world have a great interest in the story of the Assyrian assault on Lachish. It is one of the few Bible events supported and enhanced by information from multiple ancient sources, including the Bible, archaeological remains at Lachish, a contemporary written account by the Assyrians, and a depiction of the event in Assyrian art. When put together, the information provides the answers to two critical questions: Why did Assyria attack such a massive fortification so far away from their main target, Jerusalem? And why did Jerusalem's King Hezekiah respond to the fall of Lachish in such desperate fashion? The answer lies in the size of the city. If you could defeat Lachish, you were sending this unmistakable message: no city in Israel was safe. That is why Assyria attacked this imposing target. When Lachish fell, arrogance filled the language of the Assyrian envoy sent to disrupt the confidence of those living in Jerusalem (2 Chron. 32:9–15). When it fell, Sennacherib dedicated seventy feet of wall relief space in the entry hall of his palace at Nineveh to boast of his accomplishment. When it fell, Hezekiah tried to quench Sennacherib's thirst for conquest with a large tribute payment (2 Kings 18:13–16).

INFORMATION 📍 take Highway 35 southwest from Beit Guv-rin to Road 3415; watch for the entrance to Tel Lachish; 🚫

Makhtesh Ramon

The view into the Makhtesh Ramon provides one of the most breath-taking views in Israel, a place to marvel at the handiwork of the divine architect, capture the meaning of wilderness, and appreciate the Lord's provision for Israel.

A number of these *makhteshim* exist in southern Israel. In He-brew, a *makhtesh* is the bowl used in combination with a pestle for grinding. Geologists who looked at these eroded valleys enclosed within a steep set of walls thought they looked a bit like such a bowl, hence their unique name. Makhtesh Ramon is the largest of this geologic family: twenty-five miles long, six miles wide, and 2,400 feet deep.

Plan your visit so that you can walk along the edge of the crater at sunset to enjoy its colors at their most vibrant. Glowing reds, yellows, and oranges contrast sharply with the black remains of ancient volca-noes. It is also the time of day you are most likely to be accompanied by the local ibex. If you arrive early, you can spend time in the visitor center, which for a fee will help you learn more about the geology and natural history of the crater. Near the visitor center and again for a fee, the Bio Ramon wildlife park gives you a chance to learn more about wilderness animals.

The view from the crater's edge teaches what wilderness is and what it can do. After their time at Mount Sinai, the Lord led his chosen people north to the promised land through trackless wilderness like this. Jeremiah offers a definition of wilderness and a lesson involving wilderness travel in 2:5–7. As this prophet compared the challenge of being in the wilderness with the blessing of being in the promised land, he invited his readers to consider the harsh landscape through which the Lord had led his people before arriving in the promised land. The Lord led them "through the barren wilderness, through a land of deserts and ravines, a land of drought and utter darkness, a land where no one travels and no one lives" (Jer. 2:6). This is a land in which mortals could not survive, but it was an ecosystem the Lord used to humble Israel, test them, and teach them that the One who created this stunning landscape could also provide the food necessary for survival here (Deut. 8:1–3). That makes this view both one of the most stunning and one of the most educational in Israel, a view that invites you to capture what the biblical authors had in mind when they used the term "wilderness" and what the Lord had in mind by bringing Israel here.

INFORMATION 📍 just east of Mitzpe Ramon, south of Beer Sheba on Highway 40; 🚫 admission to the site is free; fees for the visitor center and the wildlife park.

⭐ Masada National Park

Natural beauty, stunning architecture, and human tragedy collide on the mesa called Masada. Softer limestone cliffs eroded away, leaving this stone mesa rising 1,300 feet above its surroundings and guarded by sheer rock walls. Its name means "fortress," and that is the role it played for both Herod the Great and the Jewish resisters who held out here during the First Jewish Revolt against Rome. There is more to see here than time may permit, so this summary will focus on the key elements found on the northern portion of the mesa.

Herod the Great is responsible for the majority of the remains you can see atop this forty-acre mesa. He used the natural defenses of the butte as the foundation for a luxury palace and lookout station that doubled as a safe house to which he could flee if his relationship deteriorated either with his Jewish subjects or with his Roman patrons. The Western Palace was the first royal residence built here. While local soil and rock composed the inner walls, their exterior was covered with plaster in an effort to simulate marble. If you like mosaics, some of the most exquisite are preserved here. While ordinary folks made do with dirt floors, Herod installed mosaic floors like those preserved in the inner rooms of the Western Palace. Eventually Herod built a second royal palace on the north side of Masada, where afternoon shade promised cooler temperatures. The three-tiered Northern Palace seems to defy gravity, clinging to the northern ledge of the butte, extending into thin air like a ship's prow into the sea. The top tier of the palace was a residence that included a curving balcony with a stunning view. The rounded second tier and rectangular third tier provided areas for entertainment and relaxation. You can reach both by descending on a modern flight of stairs. Just to the south of the Northern Palace is a very well-preserved Roman bathhouse. You can walk through the multiple rooms as the ancients did, starting in the changing room and then moving through a series of rooms, each of which offered a bathing experience warmer than the last.

But Masada was about more than luxury; it was about survival. Toward that end, much of the forty-acre mesa was farmland used to grow food. On the perimeter of the grain fields you will find columbaria. These were artificial roosts that provided habitat for doves that could be eaten and whose dung was used to fertilize the farm fields. Twenty-nine long storage rooms located on the north side of the mesa could secure a large food supply. But water remained an issue. No well or spring served Masada. Consequently, Herod built a rainwater collection system that consisted of eighteen cisterns with a storage capacity of 1.4 million cubic feet. The natural defense, food, and water available at Masada made it the perfect place to survive during a siege. And that was just what drew the Jewish resisters to it during the First Jewish Revolt against Rome.

After the Romans defeated Jerusalem in AD 70, some of the Jewish soldiers fled to Masada. After obtaining control of the place, they converted portions of it for their religious needs. This was the era in which the synagogue and *mikvah* (ritual bathing station) were added to the architecture of Masada. When Rome showed up in AD 72, they showed up in force. The Roman general, Silva, ordered the construction of a ten-foot wall that encircled Masada, cutting off supply or flight. He then brought fifteen thousand soldiers into the arena and housed them in eight square, stone-lined camps. You can still see the remains of the wall and camps at the base of the mesa. Knowing that the 967 Jewish men, women, and children could hold out against them for a long time, Silva initiated the construction of a siege ramp on the west side of Masada to bring his battering ram and mobile assault tower to bear on the defensive walls. As the Roman soldiers made final preparations for the assault on Masada, the Jewish families agreed to an unthinkable plan. Each father would end the lives of his family members, ten men were chosen to kill the surviving fathers, and one individual (chosen by lot) would execute the nine before taking his own life. That is how the plan unfolded as told by the first-century Jewish historian Josephus. It is the powerful story that lives in the archaeological remains. And it is the story that informs the spirit of Jewish nationalism, which asserts that Masada will never fall again.

You may be disappointed to learn that this historically rich place is not home to a single Bible event. We do not know if some of the Jewish fighters who held out at Masada were believers in Jesus. But there is one way the disturbing story of this place informs our Bible reading. It illuminates the world in which the early Christian church matured. When Rome dominated a region, it expected those living there to show allegiance by adopting the worship of pagan deities linked to Roman rule. This demand raised a question for those at Masada, and one that confronted Jewish believers in Jesus throughout the Roman world: How may we best live or die when faced by a dominating power that demands allegiance to other gods? That is the arresting question against which to weigh the decision made at Masada. And it is the question that informs the encouragement and direction we find in the letters of our New Testament.

> **INFORMATION** 📍 follow Highway 1 east from Jerusalem and then Highway 90 south along the Dead Sea to the entrance; 🚠 fee both for entrance and for use of the cable car if you choose not to walk to or from the summit.

Neot Kedumim Park

Neot Kedumim Park is a biblical landscape reserve. Much of the natural world in Israel is now paved or built on in a way that obscures how the land looked in Bible times. This 620-acre park works to turn back the clock so that modern visitors can see how the land of the Bible looked in an earlier era.

As a visitor you have a number of options. If you prefer a more structured experience, Neot Kedumim Park offers more intensive workshops and guided tours. Alternatively, if you prefer to wander on your own at a pace that fits your need for reflection, a number of self-guided routes are available. No matter how you choose to explore this park, you will have the chance to see and learn about the plants, trees, and animals of this land. In addition, you will find reconstructions of a cistern, water wheel, winepress, watchtower, threshing floor, and olive presses.

While learning about the natural history and culture of the past has value in itself, the park offers something more for Bible readers. The Lord chose to share his thoughts with us through the experiences of mortals living in a particular time and place. The biblical authors were familiar with the natural history and cultural installations found in this park. These are, in part, the lens through which we view the thoughts of the Almighty. Consequently, anything we can do to become more familiar with the world of the Bible will make its contents more familiar and its pages more intelligible.

INFORMATION 📍 along Route 443 between Tel Aviv and Jerusalem; 📱

⭐ Qumran National Park

The storied ruin at Qumran is much smaller and less assuming than many expect. You can compensate by knowing what to look for when exploring the archaeology and how to connect this site to the Dead Sea Scrolls, the Essenes, and your Bible reading.

Look for three things that make the archaeology of Qumran unique. First, pay attention to all the elements of the site connected with water. You will find water conduits, cisterns, and ritual purification baths scattered throughout the ruin that together form a water system that holds nearly three million gallons. This is far more water storage than would be necessary to meet the expected water needs of the few working here. Second, look for the room connected with writing, the so-called scriptorium or copying room. Although archaeologists did not find scrolls here, those living here had a great interest in copying manuscripts. The scriptorium is empty now, but when discovered, it contained long, plastered benches, inkwells, and pens. These betray its purpose as a copying room in which a reader would read a text aloud so that it could be copied by those sitting at the writing benches. Third, note that the ruin is a complex of workstations without residential facilities. The assumption is that those who worked at Qumran lived in tents around the ruin or in the many caves that dot the slopes and used the archaeological site as a work and meeting area.

The documents known collectively as the Dead Sea Scrolls were discovered in eleven of the caves in the area. The first scrolls came to light in 1947, extracted from Cave 1. (Each of the Dead Sea Scroll caves is numbered in the order of manuscript discovery.) The most accessible and photogenic is Cave 4, which you can see from the viewpoint on the southwest side of the site. The entire collection of scrolls generally falls into three categories. About 25 percent are copies of the Hebrew Bible / Old Testament that date from the third century BC. The remaining 75 percent are commentaries on the Bible or sectarian literature—that is, literature that defined the unique worldview and the lifestyle of the scrolls' writers. Given the proximity of the caves to the ruin, the evidence for writing at the ruin, and the similarities between the ceramic jars found in the ruin and those in which the scrolls were found, most scholars believe that the Dead Sea Scrolls originated at the ruin of Qumran.

But who lived in the ruin, and what were they doing here? Pliny the Elder mentions a group of Jewish separatists who moved to the west shore of the Dead Sea. He called them Essenes. While this group is not mentioned by name in the Bible, works by two other first-century writers (Josephus and Philo) do mention them. The scrolls these separatists left behind offer additional help in understanding who these people were. Some of the Essenes left Jerusalem under the leadership of the "Teacher of Righteousness," believing that the priests in Jerusalem had corrupted worship at the temple. Retreating from others, they held their possessions in common and lived in strict ritual purity while awaiting the coming of a messiah and the end of time.

Some have connected John the Baptist to the Essenes at Qumran. It is easy to see why. Both were active in approximately the same area at the same time. Both emphasized the ritual use of water and believed they were carrying out preparations for the one who would be coming in fulfillment of Isaiah 40:3–4. Despite these similarities, John's teachings and his preparations for the coming Messiah were very different from those of the Essenes. That in no way diminishes the important contributions the ruin at Qumran and the Dead Sea Scrolls offer readers of the Old and New Testaments.

The Old Testament text we have at Qumran is over 1,150 years earlier than the oldest complete Hebrew manuscript we have of the Old Testament. This is a real treasure that transports back in time by centuries our understanding of how the Hebrew Bible looked. The other literature and evidence from Qumran provide a window into the world of the New Testament. When Jesus walked this earth, he did not speak into a cultural vacuum but rather into the cultural world of the first century AD. A segment of that culture was defined by those who lived and thought like the Essenes who lived here and authored and copied the Dead Sea Scrolls. That means we will better understand some of what Jesus said in light of the view into first-century culture offered here.

INFORMATION 📍 take Highway 1 east from Jerusalem and turn south on Highway 90 in the direction of the Dead Sea; the entrance to the park is on Highway 90; 🅱️

Timna Valley National Park

Timna Valley National Park preserves a beautiful desert valley surrounded by multicolored mountains. This valley was mined for copper in Bible times, so it is the place to see the remains of ancient copper mines and understand how metals were processed and used in Bible times. But Bible readers will also benefit from the life-size replica of the Israelite tabernacle, which is also part of this park.

You will have many stops to explore within the park's fifteen thousand acres. Wherever you travel, know that the scenery is at its best in the early morning or late afternoon. These are the times of day that the sandstone columns, unusual rock formations, natural arches, and mountainsides glow with rich pastels. The ibex, oryx, and ostrich call this place home. They have been here a long time, as indicated by the Egyptian hunting scene called "The Chariots" etched into a limestone cliff on the north side of the park. It dates to the time of the Israelite judges (thirteenth to twelfth century BC).

The sandstone contained copper ore, which drew ancient miners to the valley. The remains of some ten thousand mine shafts and a variety of smelting camps dot the valley floor. A number of the parking areas provide access to these historical features of the park, giving you an opportunity to see how this important metal was harvested and processed for use. Copper was combined with tin to make bronze, a metal used from the time of Abraham to the time of the judges for making tools, weapons, and art. The mines here thrived under Egyptian and Midianite control when the judges ruled in Israel. Solomon mined the area in the tenth century BC.

Two religious installations are worthy of mention. The first is the Hathor temple, located at the foot of Solomon's Pillars on the south side of the park. This temple operated during the time of the Israelite judges. The natural sandstone pillars provide a dramatic backdrop for the temple of the Egyptian goddess Hathor, who was believed to look after the well-being of the miners. When the Midianites took over the mining operation, they established a sanctuary on the same site, apparently erecting a tent over the same sanctuary footprint. Earlier, Israel had passed through this area as they moved from Mount Sinai toward the promised land. They also had a tent sanctuary, the tabernacle. Before Solomon built a temple in Jerusalem out of stone and wood, the Lord traveled with his chosen people and made his presence known in a unique way at this portable tent sanctuary. In the area of Solomon's Pillars, you have the chance to see and explore a life-size replica of the tabernacle as it is described in the Old Testament (Exod. 26:1–27:19).

INFORMATION

📍 seventeen miles north of Eilat on Highway 90; 🚗

5

Central Mountains
CENTER

You can visit many of the places in the central portion of the central mountain zone with a day trip from Jerusalem using Highway 60. This road generally follows the path of the biblical Ridge Route. It remains one of the most scenic rural drives you can make in this land. As you travel north from Jerusalem, watch for the geography to change around you. The mountains will become lower in elevation, the severity of the slopes will diminish, and the valley systems will widen. Rainfall increases as you move north. This ripens the grain growing in the valleys and matures the olive trees that fill the terraced slopes.

In the Old Testament this was the tribal territory of Ephraim and Manasseh, the heart of what became known as the northern kingdom

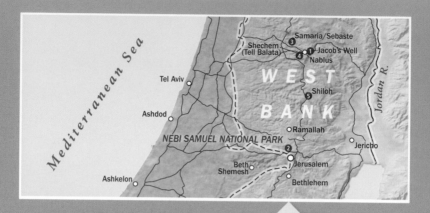

1 Jacob's Well
2 Nebi Samuel National Park
3 Samaria/Sebaste
4 Shechem (Tell Balata)
5 Shiloh

of Israel. In the New Testament this was the Roman district of Samaria and home to the Samaritans. Today it is the West Bank, home to Palestinian cities and villages. Although there are comparatively fewer stops to make in this portion of the central mountain zone and although the sites are less developed for tourists, you will see a land less obscured by modern infrastructure and visit sites that offer precious insights into familiar Bible stories.

⭐ Jacob's Well

Jesus was always the Messiah but rarely referred to himself using this title. That makes Jacob's Well special. Here Jesus verbally declared he was the Messiah while visiting with a Samaritan woman. In Jesus's day the well was not located in a building, but today it resides within the Greek Orthodox Church of Saint Photina. (If the door to the complex is closed, ring the bell for entry.)

This location has a long history. Jacob fled to Paddan Aram after tricking his brother into surrendering his birthright. When Jacob returned from Paddan Aram, he camped near the ancient city of

Shechem (Gen. 33:18–20), today's Tel Balata (discussed below), located in the mountain pass between Mount Gerizim and Mount Ebal. After purchasing a plot of ground, he dug a well here, likely because all the springs had been claimed by the locals. This well became known as Jacob's Well. Centuries later Jesus met with a Samaritan woman at this well to talk about her life, eternal life, and his identity as the Messiah (John 4:1–26). That made it a spot worth remembering. Byzantine Christians built a church over the well in the fourth century AD. The Crusaders replaced it with a church of their own in the twelfth century AD. The footprint of the Crusader church became the footprint of the modern church completed in 2007.

When you are inside the beautifully decorated modern church, look for the set of stairs at the front of the building, which will take you under the altar and into the small chapel that surrounds the well itself. The modern limestone cap, bucket, and pulley system cover a 7.5-foot-wide shaft whose depth has been variously reported from 240 feet (seventh century AD) to the more recently reported 67 feet. If you would like to take some water home, there is a small shop next to the well that will help you with that.

Christians have come to the well for thousands of years because Jesus verbally declared that he was the Messiah here (John 4:25–26). You may consider this surprising given that this well served the village of Sychar in Samaria, north of the Jewish heartland of Judea. The Samaritans who lived here descended from the non-Jewish people brought into this area by the Assyrians. Their story is told in 2 Kings 17:24–40. This non-Jewish group married into Jewish families, forming the Samaritan population of Jesus's day that held some but not all the views of the Jews of Galilee and Judea. They worshiped the Lord and expected a coming messiah but recognized only the first five books of the Old Testament as their holy writings. Mount Gerizim rather than Mount Zion was their holy mountain.

Why would Jesus come here to make a declaration like this? It likely has to do with Old Testament expectation rooted in this place. Jacob's Well lies just a short distance from the Old Testament site of Shechem. A series of Old Testament events made this a place of messianic expectation. At Shechem the Lord appeared to Abram and told him that he had arrived in the promised land (Gen. 12:6–7). That promise was intimately linked to the mission of his family, bringing the world its Savior from sin (Gen. 12:1–3). On two later occasions Joshua brought the tribes of Israel to the pass between Mount Ebal and Mount Gerizim to review their national mission in light of bringing the Messiah into the world (Josh. 8:30–35; 24:1–27). Long before the Samaritans existed, long before Jerusalem and Shiloh (discussed below) became important religious centers, there was Shechem. It was the place God's people of the past came to think about a coming Savior from sin. When we see Jacob's Well in that light, it was not just helpful for Jesus to come here and declare himself to be the Messiah; it was a place Jesus "had to go" (John 4:4).

INFORMATION 📍 east side of modern Nablus; 🚫 donations are appreciated; 🕐

⭐ Nebi Samuel National Park

A sixth-century tradition identifies this ridge with Ramah, the village in which the great Old Testament prophet Samuel was born, ministered, and was buried (1 Sam. 1:19; 7:17; 25:1). The accuracy of this tradition is in doubt, as is the true identity of this location. Scholars have associated this ridge with a variety of Bible places including Ramah, Mizpah, and the high place of Gibeon. Don't let their uncertainty and the doubtfulness of the tradition linking this to Samuel's tomb trouble you. The real value in being here has less to do with what the place is than what you can see from here. The park offers one of the best views for orienting yourself to the greater Jerusalem area and the critical piece of real estate known as the Benjamin Plateau. The label may be new to you. But if you come to understand this location, you will read a number of Old Testament stories in a new way.

Let's start with the archaeology. The large structure in front of you had its beginning in the Crusader period but achieved its current form in 1911. It marks the traditional location of Samuel's tomb and functions as both a synagogue and a mosque, given the importance of Samuel in both the Jewish and Muslim faith traditions. You will find archaeology from a variety of periods at the base of this building. To the east you will see a Crusader quarry that was turned into a stable. To the south are the remains of a Jewish village from the Hasmonean era (second century BC, between the time of the Old and New Testaments). Among the Hasmonean ruins is also evidence of Israelite settlement from the time of the divided kingdom (eighth to seventh century BC). To the west there are more remains of the Crusader fortress.

The archaeology has less to offer a Bible reader here than the view. If time is short, move quickly to the roof of the mosque. You can get there using a set of stairs accessed just inside the south entrance of the building. And don't forget to bring along a map. It will help you make sense of what you can see and orient yourself to places that lie out of sight beyond the horizon. From the roof, start by looking to the south. You will see Jerusalem and the extended ridge of the Mount of Olives. To the east you will be looking in the direction of Gibeah, Jericho, and the Jordan River. (Gibeah is the only one of the three in sight and can be identified by looking for the girders of a partially completed building on a distant ridge.) To the west beyond the plateau you will be looking toward the Aijalon Valley, the coastal plain, and the Mediterranean Sea. But the most significant view is the one to the north. In this direction you will see the Benjamin Plateau, the ancient site of Gibeon in the near foreground, and the modern city of Ramallah beyond.

Locations mentioned in the Bible that look so similar on the page have varying degrees of strategic value. Read that sentence one more time. Then look north onto the plateau. You are looking at one of the most strategic pieces of real estate in the promised land. Its value has to do with transportation, the economic well-being of Jerusalem, and the security of the central mountain region.

Start by thinking about transportation and economics. It was very difficult to move east and west through the central mountain zone. A series of north–south mountain ridges blocked the traveler's progress, turning what would have been a modest east–west walk into days of mountain climbing. But the Benjamin Plateau offered a solution. Here a high plateau interrupted the mountains and allowed an east–west crossing without all the climbing. Consequently, those moving from the Jordan River valley to the Mediterranean Sea used this route, a route we call the Jericho–Gezer Road because it connected those two cities. This was the way in which the world markets gained access to Jerusalem and the way in which Jerusalem gained access to the world markets.

Now add the security of the central mountains to the picture. Armies traveled to Jerusalem in the same way that merchants did. Throughout all periods of the Bible, those who attacked Jerusalem did so by using this route. But it was not just the security of Jerusalem but also the entire mountain interior that was in play. To see that, add the main north–south road through the mountains of Israel, the Ridge Route. It crossed this plateau just to the east of your current position at Gibeah. Put those two road systems on the landscape and you will see that the Benjamin Plateau hosted the internal crossroads of the central mountain zone. The one who controlled this plateau controlled access to and movement through this entire region. That makes the Benjamin Plateau one of the most critical pieces of property in the promised land.

Not surprisingly, the plateau is frequently alluded to in the Bible. Start with the Israelite invasion of Canaan at the time of Joshua. The invasion route is defined by place names like Jericho, Bethel, Ai, Gibeon, and Jerusalem (Josh. 6–10). When you line them up on the landscape, you are tracing a route that travels through the Benjamin Plateau. Think of what that means strategically. When Joshua and the Israelites came to control this plateau, they controlled the internal crossroads of Canaan and could prevent effective communication and the movement of goods between enemy centers to the north and south. This put them in a position to divide and conquer the Canaanite city-states north and south of the plateau. Given the location's value, you would expect Israel to conquer and occupy every village and town on the plateau. That is what makes Gibeon such a surprise. This city was not conquered, and a full chapter is dedicated to explaining this unexpected turn of events (Josh. 9). It is also why the Lord used a miracle on this plateau to give the Israelites a decisive victory over a Canaanite coalition of five southern city-states. He made sure that nothing beyond Gibeon remained in Canaanite hands (Josh. 10).

The story of this plateau continues beyond Joshua into 1 and 2 Samuel. As Samuel gathered the Israelites for a service of rededication at Mizpah, the Philistines showed up. Once again this vital real estate was threatened. But rather than discontinue the worship service, the people trusted the Lord. He responded with miraculous peals of thunder that panicked the invaders and preserved Israel's ownership of the plateau (1 Sam. 7). At the time of Solomon and before the temple was built in Jerusalem, the Israelites set up the tabernacle and great altar just to your north at Gibeon (2 Chron. 1:3–12). Its location on the plateau created access to the sanctuary via roads that radiated from here into all corners of Solomon's kingdom, assuring that all the Lord's people could get to his house.

The strategic value of places mentioned in the Bible is not always immediately evident. That is particularly true of the Benjamin Plateau and its associated towns and villages. Again and again, the biblical authors bring us to this plateau because the events that occurred here had greater importance than those occurring in other places. Understanding the significance of the plateau will open new insights and understanding into the Bible events that occurred here.

> **INFORMATION** 📍 along Highway 436 on the north side of Jerusalem; 🚫

Samaria/Sebaste

Can a location become so sinful that it cannot be redeemed? Samaria/Sebaste makes for a good test case. This isolated hill, naturally defended by its steep slopes and surrounded by a rich agricultural basin, caught the eye of Omri, the king of Israel who was in the market for a new capital city. He purchased the hill from a local man named Shemer and established a city that reflected the previous owner's name—Samaria (876 BC). It became the long-standing capital city of the northern kingdom of Israel (1 Kings 16:24). That means it also became home to the infamous couple Ahab and Jezebel. Much later Caesar Augustus gave the hill to Herod the Great, who founded a new city here (25 BC), naming it Sebaste after his patron (the Greek *Sebaste* is the equivalent of the Latin *Augusta*). Here you will have a chance to see archaeological remains from all of these historical periods and get a sense for the unique mountain geography of Manasseh. What is more, the story of Samaria/Sebaste teaches us that no place is so infamous that it cannot be redeemed by the gospel.

You will meet the archaeology in the park even before you exit your vehicle. As you drive in, you will pass round towers put in place by Herod. These guarded the western entry to the city and marked the starting point for the long, store-lined street that terminated at the city's center. The modern road follows this ancient street, which was forty-one feet wide and a half mile long and was lined with six hundred columns, some of which remain in their original place. This shopping street terminated at the main public gathering spot, the Roman forum (now partly covered by the parking area). The forum was 240 feet wide and 420 feet long, with its perimeter defined by columns.

From the parking lot, walk to the west side of the forum. Here you will find the remains of a Roman basilica, a large roofed building divided by pillars into three aisles. This was where commerce and legal proceedings of the city took place. On the north side of the basilica is a semicircular recess with stone benches, known as the exedra. This was where the magistrates of the city sat to hear legal cases. From the forum, follow the trail that begins on its eastern side to the well-preserved semicircular theater built into the side of a hill. The surviving theater dates to the second or third century AD but may well have succeeded a theater built here by Herod the Great.

Follow the trail that leads above the theater past the round Hellenistic tower, and you will come to the acropolis of Samaria/Sebaste. This high ground marks the most important part of the city in all periods. The ninety-foot-wide staircase sure to catch your eye marks the location of the Augustan temple built by Herod the Great in honor of his Roman patron. Most of the infrastructure, including the steps and altar in front of them, dates to the second-century-AD restoration of the temple accomplished by the Roman governor Septimus Severus. These later elements help provide a sense of the massive scale of the earlier temple (230 feet wide by 278 feet long). As you follow the trail along the west side of the temple, you will come to a much older wall that boasts stones cut and mated so precisely that no mortar was used to bind them together. This fine stonework is part of the palace structure at Samaria from the time of Ahab and Jezebel.

It is hard for Bible readers to find a place so steeped in infamy as this city of Samaria/Sebaste. The story begins with Omri, the founder of the city, who is characterized as more sinful than any of the kings who preceded him (1 Kings 16:25–26). Rather than focus on Israel's spiritual health and mission, Omri focused on his nation's economics. He had a plan for making his kingdom as financially prosperous as the kingdom of the Phoenicians, his neighbor to the north. This plan required diversion of merchants transporting aromatics, spices, and wool north on the King's Highway. Rather than having those goods bypass his kingdom by traveling the King's Highway on the east side of the Jordan River, he wanted them to move through his own country and then to world markets via the seaports of Phoenicia. As the middle man in this commodities trade, he stood to profit in grand fashion. To facilitate this arrangement with Phoenicia, he arranged for his son, Ahab, to marry a Phoenician princess named Jezebel.

These two pursued the economic strategy of Omri but added a theological twist to the plan. Presuming that the financial success of the Phoenicians was in large part associated with their worship of Baal, Ahab and Jezebel sought to popularize the worship of this pagan deity in their kingdom, even going so far as to build a temple to Baal here in their capital city. Ahab quickly succeeded his father in earning the title of worst of the worst kings (1 Kings 16:29–34). The Lord sent prophets to condemn this violation of the very first commandment and the rampant social injustices that followed (Jer. 23:13; Hosea 7:1–7; Amos 4:1; 6:1–7). When there was no response, the Lord allowed the invading Assyrian army to capture Samaria (2 Kings 17:6).

Centuries later this same city passed into the hands of Herod the Great, who did nothing to improve our perception of the place. While he did not champion the worship of Baal, he did champion worship of the emperor here. The temple set on the acropolis of Samaria was meant for making sacrifices to the emperor of Rome, not the Lord who had given this land to his chosen people.

The infamy of the place makes it a location to ponder. Could a city so filled with pagan infamy be redeemed? The answer comes to us in Acts 8:4–25. Philip went to "the city of Samaria" (Acts 8:5, author's translation), likely Samaria/Sebaste, to announce the life-changing message of Jesus Christ crucified and risen from the dead. When he did, the city that so long lived in infamy saw one healing miracle after the next, people baptized, and joy that only forgiven sinners can know.

When news of this reached Jerusalem, Peter and John were dispatched to the area not to correct Philip's actions but to build on them. They prayed and laid hands on the locals, who then received the Holy Spirit just like those in Jerusalem. Could this place of pagan infamy be redeemed? Absolutely!

> **INFORMATION**
> 📍 along Highway 60 near modern Sebastia; 🚫

And that becomes the enduring spiritual legacy of Samaria/Sebaste, a legacy that gives every place and every person hope, for there is no place and no person so infamous that they cannot be redeemed by the gospel.

⭐ Shechem (Tell Balata)

Shechem does not rank with places like Bethlehem, Capernaum, and Jerusalem in the minds of most Bible readers, but it should. No space in the promised land was more sacred during the early part of the Old Testament era than this. The ancient town is located in a half-mile-wide valley, beautifully framed by Mount Ebal (3,084 feet) and Mount Gerizim (2,891 feet). Given the agricultural advantages, water resources, and central location of Shechem in Canaan, this place would be expected to have a long human history. And it does, evident in the archaeology and in our Bible reading. It is where Abraham learned that Canaan was the promised land, where Joshua held services of rededication, and where King Jeroboam established the first capital city of the northern kingdom of Israel.

After spending a few minutes at the visitor center, enter the town as the ancients did through the northwest gate. On your way to the gate, you will pass a massive wall that rises thirty feet from the ground. Use your imagination to add a mud-brick wall on top of these foundation boulders and then picture this wall encircling the entire site. That is how the city looked to the one approaching it at the time Abraham's family was in the land (1650–1200 BC). A right turn through the gatehouse brings you into the city proper. Just to the north of the gatehouse is a small room with a tiny opening that allows a view of those approaching the town. The town's guards would use this peep-hole to assess the threat of a prospective visitor when the gates were closed. To the south of the gatehouse is the impressive foundation of the fortress temple (sixty-nine feet by eighty-six feet), its worship plaza, and sacred standing stone. This worship complex served the citizens of Samaria up to the time Joshua led the Israelites into the promised land and was likely the temple of Baal-Berith mentioned in Judges 9:4. Abimelek, the son of Gideon, took silver from this temple to hire reckless adventurers who helped him gain the title "king of Shechem."

Shechem is for the Old Testament what Bethlehem is for the New Testament, the start of the story. Bethlehem is the beginning of Jesus's story in the land in the same way that Shechem is the beginning of Israel's national story in this land. The Lord had promised Abram that his family-turned-nation would bless all nations of the earth in connection with a yet undisclosed land the Lord would show him (Gen. 12:1–3). When Abram arrived at Shechem, the Lord identified Canaan as the promised land. Abram honored the importance of this event by building a memorial altar here so that his family would never lose sight of this key moment in their history (Gen. 12:6–7).

That is the first important Bible story to occur here, but not the last. The biblical authors bring us to Shechem again and again. When Jacob, Abraham's grandson, returned from Paddan Aram, he purchased property near the town of Shechem, built a memorial altar of his own, and dug a well to serve those visiting this sacred spot (Gen. 33:18–20; John 4:5–6). After the extended stay in Egypt, the Lord directed Abraham's family-turned-nation to hold a service of rededication here, using the natural amphitheater formed by Mount Gerizim and Mount Ebal, to review the law that defined Israel's national mission and lifestyle (Deut. 27:1–8). When Joshua led Israel into the promised land, he brought the nation of Israel to this spot, built an altar on Mount Ebal, wrote the law code given to Moses on stones coated in plaster, and then positioned the people at the base of the twin mountains for the service of review and rededication (Josh. 8:30–35). Just a few years later, when the conquest had come to an end, Joshua brought Israel back to this same location to once again review the law and rededicate the nation to its founding principles and its mission (Josh. 24:1–27). His final impassioned speech to Israel echoed off these mountainsides: "But as for me and my household, we will serve the Lord" (Josh. 24:15). After Israel declared their passion to do the same, they buried the bones of Joseph in Shechem on the tract of land purchased by Jacob in order to fulfill the request Joseph had made before he died in Egypt (Gen. 50:25; Josh. 24:32).

If the importance of Shechem had escaped your attention, realize that it is regarded as one of the most important locations in the Old Testament era. Before Jesus was born in Bethlehem, before the temple was built in Jerusalem, before there was a sanctuary at Shiloh, there was Shechem. This becomes the place most intimately associated with the founding promises given to Abraham and the covenant made with Israel at the time of Moses. During the early part of the Old Testament, there is no more sacred space in the promised land than this. That is how the biblical authors and poets thought about

INFORMATION 📍 in the heart of modern Nablus, just north of Ramallah Road near the site of Jacob's Well; 🚫

it. And that is how Bible readers need to think about it, a place of hope, forgiveness, and expectation of all that was to come.

Shiloh

Shiloh plays a vital role in the story line of the Old Testament. Although less stellar than Shechem, it belongs near the top of a list of key biblical towns. Shiloh was home for the tabernacle, home for Samuel, and home to a legacy that Jeremiah employed in a sermon hundreds of years later. Its location is precisely defined in Judges 21:19, evidence that points us to the well-developed archaeological site of Tel Shiloh.

The ruin of Shiloh covers approximately 7.5 acres, a typical size for an Israelite town during Old Testament times. But the archaeology here is far from ordinary and begs for exploration. From the reception building walk north toward the hill on which ancient Shiloh is built. Just to the northwest of the picnic area outside the reception building you will find an ancient winepress used to extract juice from harvested grapes. Here the bedrock has been refashioned into a rectangular treading floor on which the grapes were crushed underfoot. Imagine the juice flowing by gravity from this floor through the small channels cut in the treading floor and into two square collecting pools excavated into the stone.

To the northeast of this winepress and before you get to the hill on which the ancient city was built, you will encounter the reconstruction of a Byzantine church that rises above original mosaic floors. Christians built a number of early churches here because tradition remembers this as the spot on which the tabernacle at Shiloh stood.

Continue north and climb the hill. This is where you will find the ruins of Old Testament Shiloh. It is unmistakably marked by a modern, round building that doubles as observation deck and media presentation center. Follow the path that leads along the western side of the tell, past Byzantine structures with their neatly trimmed stone, until you come to an area of fieldstones left in their natural shape on the

Israel had only one sanctuary, to remind them that they paid allegiance to only one God. The tabernacle was highly portable and had multiple zones, which imposed increasing restrictions on those approaching the innermost chamber, the place where the Lord was present in a special way.

1 Courtyard
2 Altar of burnt offering
3 Bronze basin
4 Tabernacle

west and northwest side of the hill. The more substantial wall dates to the seventeenth century BC, when Abraham's family was in Egypt. This is the Canaanite defensive wall that encircled their 4.2-acre city perched on top of the hill. In its day, this perimeter wall stood twenty-four feet tall and in places grew to eighteen feet wide! It was complemented by a sloping ramp of earth (a glacis) outside the city wall. This glacis was eighty-two feet wide at the bottom and pitched at twenty-five degrees. This open slope below the wall made it difficult for attackers to find any protection from the defenders shooting arrows at them from the top of the wall. Although the battle is not recorded in Joshua, the Israelites overcame these defenses and took possession of the town. Ironically they did not rebuild or reuse the Canaanite defensive works. Instead, the Israelites built their homes and storehouses through and outside of the earlier defensive works. Of particular note are the storage rooms in which archaeologists found large ceramic storage jars. This complex of rooms is presumed to be a set of auxiliary buildings that provided storage for the supplies used at the tabernacle when it was here.

Multiple layers of material were draped over a wood-framed structure to create the tabernacle proper (30 feet long and 15 feet wide), which was divided into two rooms: the holy place and the most holy place. The outer layers were weather resistant, while the interior layer provided color and design. Access to the interior of the tabernacle was denied to all but Israel's priests. There are two possible locations for the tabernacle. The first is the area south of the tell on which the Byzantine churches were built. The second is on the north side of the archaeological site where a rectangular plateau with an east–west orientation conforms to the necessary dimensions of the tabernacle courtyard. You can get a nice view of this plateau from the deck of the round visitor center.

As Bible readers, the first impressions we have of Shiloh are warm and positive, associated with the tabernacle and land division. Joshua erected the tabernacle here because this small hill was centrally located in the promised land and accessible to all the tribes via the Ridge Route. The tabernacle remained here until the time of Eli (Josh. 18:1). After Joshua had led the Israelite army to victory over all the major city-states in Canaan, it was time to divide the remaining land among the tribes that had not yet received a land parcel. This took place at Shiloh, the religious center, because land division had a religious as well as a practical dimension. The land these families farmed and used to pasture their livestock was their part of the promised land that reminded them of the Lord's promise to send a Savior from sin. Consequently, the final land division started and ended in Shiloh. From here Joshua sent teams to survey the land. When they returned, the reports combined with the casting of lots saw to it that each tribe received a land parcel that fit who they were and where the Lord wanted them to be (Josh. 18:1–10).

However, the good feelings associated with Shiloh quickly fade when we begin reading 1 Samuel. The young boy Samuel was here. His humble words to the Lord, "Speak, for your servant is listening" (1 Sam. 3:10), stand in sharp contrast to the religious leaders at Shiloh, who were doing anything but listening to the Lord (1 Sam. 2:12–17, 22–25). As a result, the Lord allowed the Philistine army to ransack the place and bring harm to the very sanctuary Joshua had erected here. The good feelings associated with Shiloh turned to disdain. And the memory of the land division faded into a new lesson taught by Shiloh: personal disregard for the Lord by his worship leaders and thoughtless worship by his people are offenses so serious that they result in the Lord allowing his own sanctuary to be ransacked.

It is in this light that Jeremiah mentions Shiloh hundreds of years later. By this time Solomon had built a permanent temple for the Lord in Jerusalem. The faithfulness of God's people faded again despite Jeremiah's passionate pleas for a change of heart. He even warned the people of Jerusalem that the Lord would allow the holy city and its sanctuary to be destroyed by the advancing Babylonian army if they failed to repent. Instead of repenting, the people countered with these words: "This is the temple of the LORD, the temple of the LORD, the temple of the LORD!" (Jer. 7:4). The popular assumption was that the Lord would never allow Jerusalem and the Lord's sanctuary to face harm. In response, Jeremiah urged them to consider Shiloh and what the Lord had done to his sanctuary there at the time of Eli (Jer. 7:12–15). Here the Lord taught an important lesson that lingers to this day on the landscape: it is better for the Lord's sanctuary to lie in ruin than for it to endure with corrupt leadership and thoughtless worship.

INFORMATION 📍 within the modern Jewish settlement of Shilo, about thirty-two kilometers north of Jerusalem on Highway 60; 🌐

6

Central Mountains
NORTH

The evolving character of the central mountains continues as you make your way into the northernmost portion of this zone. Traveling from south to north, you will first meet the sprawling Jezreel Valley, where the mountains of this zone give way to an expansive plain. This plain offers nutrient-rich soils for growing grain and the best east–west route of passage through the promised land, a route used by merchants and soldiers alike. As expected, important cities sprang up along its perimeter, places with an international orientation like Jezreel and Megiddo. Lower Galilee lies immediately north of the Jezreel Valley and marks a return to the mountainous nature of this zone. Lower Galilee consists of a series of east–west ridges and valleys.

Mediterranean Sea

LEBANON

SYRIA

Mt. Hermon

GOLAN HEIGHTS

KORAZIM NATIONAL PARK (Chorazin)

Mount of Beatitudes

SEPPHORIS (ZIPPORI NATIONAL PARK)

Haifa

Gamla Nature Reserve

Sea of Galilee

KURSI NATIONAL PARK

Mt. Carmel

Mt. Tabor

Mt. Precipice (Nazareth)

MOUNT ARBEL NATIONAL PARK AND NATURE RESERVE

MEGIDDO NATIONAL PARK

Jezreel Valley

BETH SHEAN NATIONAL PARK

1 Banias (Paneas, Caesarea Philippi)	**13** Korazim National Park (Chorazin)
2 Beth Shean National Park	**14** Kursi National Park
3 Bethsaida (Julias)	**15** Megiddo
4 Capernaum	**16** Mount Arbel National Park and Nature Reserve
5 Dan	**17** Mount of the Beatitudes
6 En Harod	**18** Mount Precipice (Nazareth)
7 Gamla Nature Reserve	**19** Mukhraqa Monastery on Mount Carmel
8 Har Bental (Mount Bental)	**20** Mount Tabor
9 Hazor	**21** Nazareth
10 Heptapegon (Tabgha)	**22** Sea of Galilee
11 Jezreel	**23** Sepphoris (Zippori National Park)
12 Katzrin Historic Village	

These valleys are fit for farming and produced food for the people living in Lower Galilee's many towns and villages. As the name suggests, Lower Galilee is lower in elevation but ranks high in Gospel stories. It was where Jesus spent the great majority of his time on earth. This is where you will find his hometown, Nazareth, and the home base for his ministry, Capernaum. To the north of Lower Galilee is Upper Galilee. It is higher in elevation, harder to farm, and less populated. It is a great region for backcountry hiking, but it hosted few Bible stories.

✪ Banias (Paneas, Caesarea Philippi)

Natural beauty and Bible insight come together at the Greco-Roman city known as Caesarea Philippi during the time of Jesus. You will find the remains of this city and its pagan sanctuary within the Hermon Stream Nature Reserve. This reserve offers a variety of hiking trails that will connect you to the archaeology and natural history of northern Israel. During Jesus's days, gentiles lived here and worshiped their pagan deities at the base of the cliff ahead of you. Against that backdrop, Jesus began a conversation with the disciples about who he was and what he was capable of doing that quickly turned into a conversation about who they were and what they were capable of doing.

You will meet the archaeology even before you exit your vehicle. As you drive into the reserve, you will pass through the middle of a palace complex built here by Herod the Great's grandson, Agrippa II. When you park, note the ruins located on the south side of the parking lot. This is the ornate entry to the worship area you are about to visit, built by Herod's son Philip. He gained possession of this city following the death of his father and made it his regional capital (2 BC).

From the parking lot, walk toward the flowing water, the massive stone cliff (230 feet long and 131 feet tall), and the yawning cave (66 feet wide and 49 feet tall) that attracted the first visitors to this site. This colorful cliff is actually the southernmost ridge of Mount Hermon, the highest mountain in the region, which looms out of sight above you and to the north. During Bible times the cave was the exit point for a powerful spring gushing water at a rate of more than 5,200 gallons per second. (Because of a shift in the subsurface geology, the spring now discharges its water below the cave rather than through the cave.) The water flowing from this spring into the pools before you is the start of the Hermon Stream, one of the three tributaries that join to become the Jordan River.

The combination of water, cave, and cliff gives this setting an otherworldly look and feel, so it is not surprising that shortly after the last book of the Old Testament was written (in the Hellenistic era), this became a place of pagan worship. Here gentiles worshiped the Greek god Pan, whose idol stood in one of the niches cut into the cliff face. Pan is the half-man, half-goat deity associated with shepherds and the natural world whose worship gave this place its first name, Paneas (Arabic, Banias). The eerie flow of water from the cave further reminded these ancient worshipers of the river Styx, which formed the boundary between earth and the underworld. Consequently, the gaping cave spewing water was associated with the gateway to the underworld, Hades. As time passed, other deities were honored here and other temples came to line the cliff face. In Jesus's day, this included a temple built to honor Caesar Augustus. In 20 BC Augustus added this area to the territorial holdings of Herod the Great, who was quick to honor his patron with an imperial temple built in front of the cave. Only a few elements of the masonry remain from this structure, which you can see immediately to the left (west) of the cave.

Jesus spent very little time in this far northern area that was predominantly gentile and overwhelmingly pagan in orientation. Yet he made one very important trip here. He came to have a conversation about who he was and what he could do. This conversation helped prepare the disciples for difficult days ahead, because from here Jesus initiated his last trip to Jerusalem (Matt. 16:13–20). As they entered the region of Caesarea Philippi, Jesus asked his disciples what others thought about him. This quickly turned to the pointed question, "What about you? Who do you say I am?" You may hear a question about identity. But in the ancient world, who you were was intimately linked to what you could do. That means Jesus's question and Simon Peter's answer were addressing not just Jesus's identity but also his capability. Simon Peter declared, "You are the Messiah, the Son of the living God," and so capable of anything! This lesson was of critical importance. But there was more to learn here. Jesus wanted the disciples to realize who they were and what they could do. As a master teacher, Jesus used the setting not only to make the point but also to make the point memorable. Because of Simon's stellar confession, Jesus gave him the name Peter, "the rock," or better here "the cliff," like the cliff that formed the backdrop for the pagan sanctuary at Caesarea. Not just Peter but all those who believe in Jesus as their Savior become like this cliff, like Mount Hermon, which perpetually and powerfully dominates the landscape. If the church is built on this foundation, nothing will be able to overcome it, not even the paganism that so dominated the ancient world and this cliff face. As Jesus put it, "And the gates of Hades will not overcome it."

INFORMATION 📍 the best touring options start at the Banias Springs parking area, accessed by traveling on Highway 99 east of Qiryat Shemona; 🚻

⭐ Beth Shean National Park

This park offers the most complete reconstruction of an ancient Roman city in Israel. That makes it the best place to understand the physical appearance of a New Testament–era Decapolis city and to appreciate the way in which its design was meant to influence the way the locals thought about Roman culture and religion. It is also the place to appreciate this simple fact: the founding and growth of the Christian church was an absolute miracle. It occurred in the face of pagan worship apparently affirmed by this kind of architecture.

People have lived here continuously for nearly six thousand years. From the sixteenth to the twelfth century BC (from the time of end of the sojourn in Egypt to the time of Joshua and Judges), Egyptians had an administrative center here. The Philistines and Israelites followed in turn during the eleventh and tenth centuries BC (the time of the united kingdom). These early adopters of Beth Shean built their city on the high ground, the natural hill turned archaeological tell that rises 260 feet behind the Roman city.

What accounts for the long history of this place? Beth Shean (Scythopolis) resides at the juncture of two important valleys, the north–south Jordan River valley and the east–west Jezreel Valley. The latter provided the link to world markets via the International Highway and the King's Highway of the Transjordan. It was an ideal place to observe and control movement as well as collect tariffs on trade goods. We would expect a crossroads of commerce to have a long history, and this one does.

The top of the tell is where Bible history crosses paths with this place. You can climb to the top using a set of stairs on the east side of the Roman city. But if you walk to the top of the tell, plan to be wowed more by the view than the archaeology. To the east you will have a panoramic view of the Jordan Valley and the Transjordan mountains. To the west you will be looking down into the archaeology of the Roman city. Just one Bible event occurs here. The Philistines impaled the body of Saul on the wall of their city to demonstrate the total defeat of Israel (1 Sam. 31:10). As yet there is no archaeological evidence for this wall or the Philistine city. The Bible also briefly mentions a connection between Beth Shean and Solomon (1 Kings 4:12), which is marked by archaeology. The remains of an Israelite tower can be seen on the southeast side of the upper tell.

By the third century BC (during the time between the Old and New Testaments), the focus moved to the base of the tell. Here the city of

Scythopolis was established and became a Greco-Roman Decapolis city by the second century BC. The reconstructed city that awaits your exploration has elements that date from the second to eighth century AD (well after the events recounted in the Gospels). This city includes a seven-thousand-seat theater, a bathhouse, streets engineered with a drainage system, and colonnaded, mosaic-covered sidewalks lined with shops. Water was brought into the city and distributed via a pair of public water fountains. This really changed the life of its residents who were able to go to a Roman *nymphaeum* (public water fountain) rather than make multiple trips to a water resource located outside the city. A portion of this water supply was even directed to a multiseat, indoor bathroom.

Equally striking in Scythopolis is what has been left unreconstructed, the parts of the city where we have evidence of a horrific earthquake in AD 749. The evidence is best seen at the intersection of the two main streets on the east side of the lower city. Two great tectonic plates, Arabian and African, meet in the Jordan River valley. The faster moving Arabian plate gets stuck, and tectonic tension builds. When that tension is released, the promised land experiences devastating seismic events like those mentioned in Amos 1:1 and Zechariah 14:5. Here we can see the destructive power of such quakes on an ancient city.

What is the biggest takeaway from Beth Shean for Bible readers? The reconstruction of this Roman city provides us with the best place in Israel to see the nature of a Decapolis city and to understand the rhetoric of its architecture. Decapolis cities were massive in scale compared to the towns and villages occupied by the locals. They guarded important roadways, served as administrative centers, and used their grandeur to influence the perception of the locals. The elegant buildings with their imported marble and granite components were considerably larger and more exotic than any of the indigenous, local buildings. Amenities like a *nymphaeum* and indoor bathroom provided experiences completely foreign to the locals. This made an impression, and that was the point. Rome was using such architecture to demonstrate that its society, morals, and religion were superior to anything homegrown.

When we read the New Testament stories about the growth of the early church, we may not think about cities and architecture like this. But imagine the challenge faced by the first followers of Jesus. They mainly came from the lowest rungs of the social ladder and from the most modest villages. Yet they claimed to know a better way. It is a miracle that anyone listened! But they did. Despite its theater, hot bath, and indoor toilet, Beth Shean did not address the deepest needs of the human soul. That message was carried by fishermen and farmers who came from places like Nazareth, Capernaum, and Nain. They brought a message of peace, hope, and eternal life. People at Beth Shean listened to peasants because, despite its grand architecture, their city could not fill the spiritual void in their lives in the way the gospel did.

INFORMATION 📍 within the modern city of Beit She'an, with entry off of Sha'ul HaMelech Street; 🏛

Bethsaida (Julias)

The name Bethsaida is Aramaic for "house of the fisherman." It is the third most frequently mentioned town in the Gospels. But these references can get confusing because there are actually two Bethsaidas mentioned in the Gospels, both on the north shore of the Sea of Galilee. The first is the fishing village from which Philip, Andrew, and Peter came (John 1:44). It is also called "Bethsaida in Galilee" (John 12:21). The location of this Bethsaida has not been conclusively identified, although it may be the yet unexplored Tel el-Araj, which is close to the shoreline of the Sea of Galilee and west of the Jordan River inlet. The other Bethsaida is the one we are presenting here. The Gospels use it to identify the location of several of Jesus's miracles. This is the archaeological site of Khirbet et-Tel, first-century Bethsaida Julias, the name by which it was known during the time of Herod Philip, the son of Herod the Great.

You will find three elements of its archaeology to be of interest. The ruins of two houses located in the middle of the site have a first-century connection. One is called the Wine Maker's House, because of the wine cellar within it. The other is called the Fisherman's House, because fishing gear like anchors, weights, and fishhooks and a seal depicting a cast net were found within it. South of these homes you will encounter the foundation for an Iron Age gatehouse adorned with ritual standing stones and an altar. This archaeology is likely associated with the Old Testament kingdom of Geshur. David secured the northern part of his future kingdom by marrying a royal princess of Geshur (2 Sam. 3:3). Later he nearly lost his kingdom to Absalom, a son born from this marriage (2 Sam. 13:30–38).

This is the Bethsaida of the Gospels that is put to work as a geographical reference point in locating two of Jesus's miracles: his walking on water (Mark 6:45) and the feeding of the five thousand (Luke 9:10). It is also the place where Jesus healed a blind man (Mark 8:22). This was but one of many miracles Jesus did on the streets of Bethsaida, given the strong criticism that Jesus directed at this city (Matt. 11:21; Luke 10:13). Like Chorazin and Capernaum, its residents had failed to take advantage of the opportunities Jesus had lavished on the place by spending a considerable amount of ministry time here.

INFORMATION 📍 within the Jordan River Park, just north of the Bethsaida Junction along Route 888; 🌐

⭐ Capernaum

At Capernaum you can walk where Jesus walked and sit next to structures whose stones heard his voice. There are many Capernaum stories to read because this is one of the towns in which Jesus did the majority of his teaching and miracles during his three-year ministry on earth (Matt. 11:20–24). It is called his "own town" or the "home" to which he returned (Matt. 9:1; Mark 2:1). For nearly two millennia the memory of its location has been firmly established not just by archaeology but also by Christian pilgrims who had the same passion that has fueled your trip to this land, a passion to linger where Jesus did and listen to his voice.

The first thing you notice may be the maze of low, black stone walls that fill this site. These were the homes of first-century Capernaum. Farmers, fishermen, tax collectors, and Roman soldiers lived together here and built their homes using basalt, the local stone with a volcanic past. This black stone is found throughout the lake basin, making it the most convenient stone to use when building a family living compound. But it has one important drawback. Basalt building stones more than four feet in length can crack. That meant building with shorter blocks, which led to narrower rooms. And narrower rooms led the builders to compensate by designing living compounds with large open courtyards. Put it together and you have a floor plan that consisted of an open courtyard surrounded by smaller, enclosed rooms. This became known as *insula*-style construction after the courtyard that looks like an island surrounded by a sea of rooms. The courtyard was unroofed, providing an airy setting for most of the daytime activities of the extended family members. At sunset, nuclear families could retreat to the windowless privacy of their own small room connected to the courtyard by a single door. These single-story rooms had roofs composed first of wooden rafters spanning the stone walls and then layers of reeds, grass, and mud. This is the sort of barrier that the friends of the disabled man breeched when bringing him to Jesus (Mark 2:1–12).

Two larger structures deserve particular attention in Capernaum. The first is covered by the modern church (1991) designed to look like a ship sailing on the Sea of Galilee. This building hovers above the traditional location of Peter's home (Matt. 8:14). If the gate to the church is open, walk up the stairs and into the middle of the sanctuary. There you will find a plastic window in the floor that allows you to look down into the single room of an *insula* compound identified as Peter's home. This single room expanded into a larger house church by the fourth century AD. Here early Christian visitors left behind messages scrawled in the plaster walls. These ancient graffiti make reference to Jesus and to Peter. As the popularity of Peter's home increased, the building expanded again and again. You can see the most identifiable of these early expansions by looking at the foundation on its west side. Here remains of an octagonal structure are apparent. These are the ruins of a memorial church built to mark the spot in the fifth century AD.

The second structure of importance to the story of Jesus in Capernaum is the white limestone synagogue located in the center of the compound. It dates from the fourth to fifth century AD and consists of two main rooms, the primary hall of the synagogue and a prayer hall immediately to its east. This building was destroyed in the seventh century AD, but many of the beautiful reliefs incorporated into its architecture are preserved throughout the grounds. Given the evidence, it seems best to interpret this building not as a working synagogue of this era but as a Christian monument designed to mark the importance of the building beneath it. From the west side of the white building, you will get your best view of that earlier building. Look beneath the limestone and you will see a black basalt foundation. Several things are worth noting about it. The four-foot-thick wall of the earlier building does not fully align with the wall line of the white building above it. That means the black, four-foot-thick wall had a history of its own and is not merely the foundation for the white building above. What is more, the top step leading into the synagogue on its southwest corner has been cut away so that those entering can look down and see the basalt wall of the earlier building. This and other evidence suggests that the white limestone building was built to mark the site of the black basalt building beneath it. That large public building from the first century can be none other than the very synagogue in which Jesus spent considerable time. The Romans destroyed the synagogue during the time of the First Jewish Revolt, but the memory of its location survived. This led to the construction of the white limestone synagogue precisely where the earlier building had stood.

Admittedly, there is a lot to take in here, and you may need a few moments to put it all together. The plaza near these two buildings can get crowded and noisy, but walk to the east side of the compound near the Sea of Galilee and things change. As the sound of the boisterous crowds gives way to the sound of waves gently lapping on the rocks, think about the overlap between this space and Jesus's life. Matthew tells us that he left the village of Nazareth and came to live in Capernaum (Matt. 4:13). There are a couple of reasons for this move. First, this move fulfilled Old Testament prophecy. Isaiah said that when the Messiah came to earth, he would influence two geographical locations more than others. These are the Old Testament tribal territories of Zebulun and Naphtali (Isa. 9:1–2; Matt. 4:13–16). Jesus grew up in Nazareth, a village located in Zebulun. He then moved to Capernaum, establishing a ministry base in Naphtali, bringing the prophecy of Isaiah full circle.

The second thing to note about this move of Jesus from Nazareth to Capernaum is that it put him in the public spotlight. The rural and isolated village of Nazareth limited Jesus's exposure; Capernaum created exposure. The International Highway traveled just west of Capernaum. This highway connected the Sea of Galilee basin with the world, giving everything Jesus said and did an international audience. Capernaum was where Jesus spoke regularly on the Sabbath and healed the sick and demon possessed (Matt. 8:5–13; 17:24–27; Mark 1:21–28; Luke 4:31–37). This was where Jesus called himself the "bread of life" (John 6:24–59). And now the Lord has brought you here so that you can linger where Jesus did and listen carefully to his voice as he speaks words of comfort, encouragement, and direction into your life.

INFORMATION 📍 sixteen kilometers north of Tiberias along the east side of Highway 87; 🏷 🏛

✪ Dan

The Tel Dan Nature Reserve preserves treasures for both the nature lover and the Bible student. Its name is linked to the Israelite tribe of Dan that resettled in this location and changed the name of the city in this reserve from Laish to Dan (Judg. 18:1–2, 27–29). These early settlers described the place with language that still fits. It is "a land that lacks nothing whatever" (Judg. 18:10). To sample the richness, hike as much of the 120-acre reserve as you can. Its trails wind along streams and through thick forests fed by dozens of springs. Along these trails you will see archaeological remains that include the second-oldest arched gate in Israel (1750 BC), built shortly after Jacob's family traveled to Egypt, as well as the infamous high place at Dan built at the time of King Ahab.

Follow the signs for the "long trail" to enjoy a full circuit of the park. Along this wooded trail, you will meet spring after spring carrying the melt of the winter snow that has fallen on Mount Hermon. Combined, these springs gush at a rate of more than two thousand gallons per second and coalesce to form the Dan River, whose sound will be your companion on the first part of this walk. This stream, which impatiently rushes toward the Sea of Galilee, is the most significant tributary of the upper Jordan River. Combined with the springs, this stream creates the thriving ecosystem through which you are walking with its abundance of flora and fauna, including the rare fire salamander. If you would like to learn more about the natural world of this region, the Bet Ussishkin Museum, adjacent to the reserve, has a wonderful natural history section.

The north side of the reserve contains one of the most infamous places mentioned in the Bible, the high place at Dan. Following the time of Solomon, the united kingdom of Israel divided into two political entities, the northern kingdom of Israel and the southern kingdom of Judah. During this time of political division, the Lord intended for citizens of both kingdoms to maintain a focus on their singular spiritual mission, bonded by their worship at a common place, Jerusalem. But the first king of the northern kingdom, Jeroboam, saw this plan as a threat to his own political future. Consequently, he established worship sites at Bethel and Dan, sanctuaries designed to keep his subjects away from Jerusalem and their minds off political reunification (1 Kings 12:25–30). The alternative worship conducted at Bethel and Dan employed the name of the Lord but comingled his name with pagan practices and a calf idol. This hybrid religion was part of Jeroboam's plan. He wanted to unify his Israelite and Canaanite subjects under a new national religion that blended symbols and worship from both communities. Of course, the biblical authors did not celebrate the inventiveness of Jeroboam because it undermined the very foundation laid by the first commandment. The prophets relentlessly attacked the worship at Dan, and they used it as a tool with which to evaluate all the kings that followed Jeroboam. Unfortunately, none of his successors ended the worship of the golden calf here at Dan (1 Kings 15:34; 16:26; etc.).

What remains of this infamous sanctuary? Although the calf statue has not survived and the sanctuary underwent modification after the time of Jeroboam, you can still see the raised platform made with carefully cut stones on which the temple rested. In front of the steps that lead up to this platform, you will see a replica of the original altar outlined in stainless steel (the original would have been made completely from stone). The archaeologists designed the replica and established its scale based on a stone altar horn discovered here and the set of surviving steps next to the replica altar.

Continue your walk and you will come to two gatehouses, the structures designed not just to hold up the swinging door of the city but also to provide a fortification to repulse attackers. The local geography assured they would come. The mountains to the north of Dan and swampland to the south restricted travel into and out of the promised land. Consequently, when the empires of Mesopotamia attacked this land, they did so through this geographic gateway, leading Jeremiah to write, "The snorting of the enemy's horses is heard from Dan; at the neighing of their stallions the whole land trembles" (Jer. 8:16). From one era to the next, the local residents responded by building large, fortified cities in this natural gateway. These fortified cities each had gatehouses. The surviving elements of these gatehouses provide a look into how city defenses evolved as the empires invading this region evolved their methods of attack.

Start with the Canaanite gate located on the south side of the reserve opposite the high place and underneath a modern protective cover. This is the way a city's gatehouse looked in the Middle Bronze era when Abraham's family lived in the promised land and during the first years of their stay in Egypt. Note the material used for building the gatehouse: sun-dried mud bricks. You can see how such a gate would have looked by examining the reconstructed towers on either side of the entry. Next, let your eyes follow the cobblestone steps toward the structure and you will see the physical opening of the gatehouse, an opening still filled in by soil to prevent collapse. Just above that fill, you can make out the original mud bricks laid to create an arch. Three arches like this provided support for the superstructure of the gatehouse. That makes this one of the oldest surviving arched structures in the world. Combine this gatehouse with an earthen berm that surrounded the city and you have the picture of how the fifty-acre city of Laish defended itself.

By the ninth century BC, the Assyrian battering ram could make short work of mud-brick walls, so the design plan changed. Continue down the path from the earlier gatehouse to see how city entries were built at the time of King Ahab. In this era defense structures consisted of thick walls composed of interlocked stones of various sizes (called chinking-stone construction). These walls would not collapse as a unit but had to be picked apart slowly. This was the plan. The longer you could delay the enemy at the perimeter of the promised land, the less likely they were to continue into Israel's heartland. And it was not just the construction technique but the size of the gatehouse that changed. A walk through this defensive structure at Dan shows just how large it was. The initial swinging gate of the city opened into an enclosed courtyard that housed a raised dais (platform) where the king could sit when meeting his subjects (2 Sam. 15:2). Look to the right of the raised platform for the throne and you will see the stone bench on which the city's elders sat (Prov. 31:23). A second swinging gate led from this courtyard into a massive gatehouse with opposing guard chambers on either side. The gatehouse created a bottleneck for those who wished to enter the city. In peacetime this created the opportunity for various forms of social interaction like markets and courts for legal proceedings. But during war the chambers in the gatehouse held soldiers ready to skewer enemy soldiers who tried to get past them. Beyond this gatehouse a cobbled street travels uphill, not into the city proper but to another gatehouse. Only after passing through this second structure would you be in the city itself.

This impressive defensive system had an Achilles' heel. Just outside the entrance to the first courtyard, you will see a pagan altar. This worship location was not for honoring the Lord but for worshiping three deities represented by three standing stones. This gate shrine shows that while the gate architecture had changed in Dan, its spiritual condition had not. There is no mistaking the importance of Dan to the national security of the northern kingdom. But the well-being of the promised land had more to do with uncompromised trust in the Lord than the size and composition of a gatehouse. That is why the Lord allowed Dan and the entire northern kingdom to fall before the Assyrians in the eighth century BC. And it all started here with Jeroboam, who "enticed Israel away from following the LORD and caused them to commit a great sin" (2 Kings 17:21).

INFORMATION 📍 twelve kilometers northeast of Qiryat Shemona along Highway 99; 🚗

En Harod

Ma'ayan Harod National Park is a grassy parcel of land designed for picnics, family gatherings, and camping. Located at the foot of Mount Gilboa, this pleasant park also contains a spring traditionally identified as the "spring of Harod" or the "spring of Gideon." Here two very different Bible stories come together, the story of Gideon and the story of Saul. They occur at different times and in different Bible books and involve two different leaders facing two different enemies in battles that had two very different outcomes. But they share a geographical setting. Gideon made his camp at the base of Mount Gilboa near the spring of Harod (Judg. 7:1). Saul also made his camp at the base of Mount Gilboa near the spring at Jezreel two and a half miles to the east (1 Sam. 28:4; 29:1). The geography that links these two events invites us to bring them together. In doing so, we see that the events are more similar than different. Both involve leaders of Israel wrestling with the same question: Is one God enough?

The story of Gideon occurred during the turbulent time of the judges, when the Lord intended for the individual tribes of Israel to grow in their spiritual commitment to him and to consolidate their hold on the promised land. Instead, Israel grew comfortable with its pagan neighbors, adopted the worship of their gods, and ended up losing land rather than gaining it. Sadly, many in Israel did not believe that one God was enough. That manner of thinking had consequences that were felt during the time of Gideon. Midianites, Amalekites, and other eastern peoples invaded the promised land in massive numbers (Judg. 6:1–3). They camped north of Mount Moreh in the agriculturally rich and transportation-critical Jezreel Valley (Judg. 7:1). Faithful Gideon mustered Israelite soldiers at the Harod Spring so that they could hydrate prior to entering the battle against this vast army. This was when the Lord started sending soldiers home! Eventually the Lord told Gideon to separate the soldiers by how they drank at the spring (Judg. 7:4–8), reducing his fighting force to a mere three hundred soldiers. Would that be enough? Yes! And the Lord demonstrated that when he was with them, *one God* was enough. Gideon's small band of soldiers routed the much larger enemy.

Two hundred years later we find Saul in this same area facing the final battle of his life and confronted by the same question: Is one God enough? The Philistines had invaded the Jezreel Valley, severing the northern portion of Saul's kingdom from the south. Under these grave circumstances, Saul had mustered the Israelite army at the base of Mount Gilboa near the spring of Jezreel. But there was a difference. This leader, unlike Gideon, had shown again and again that he did not think the Lord was sufficient. Even though he had Gideon's story clinging to this real estate, reminding him of God's sufficiency, Saul failed to follow Gideon's example. Instead he traveled across the valley to Mount Moreh in order to meet with a witch at Endor (1 Sam. 28:7–25). Is one God enough? Not in Saul's mind. As a result, his army was easily defeated. And at the close of the battle, the mortally wounded Saul took his own life on Mount Gilboa.

Is one God enough? The Lord wants all of us to answer this question as the psalmist did: "Whom have I in heaven but you? And earth has nothing I desire besides you. My flesh and my heart may fail, but God is the strength of my heart and my portion forever" (Ps. 73:25–26). Gideon provides the example to follow, and Saul provides the example to shun. These two stories separated in time are brought together by place. When we read them in tandem, the lesson they teach is amplified. Our one God is enough, sufficient to save in all circumstances.

INFORMATION 📍 fifteen kilometers from Afula; take Highway 71 to Road 7107; 🚗

Gamla Nature Reserve

This picturesque and peaceful reserve is home to a variety of plants and animals, harbors the highest waterfalls in Israel (167 feet), and preserves the ruins of a first-century-AD Jewish village, including the foundation of its synagogue. Few ancient synagogues have survived. So for those interested in understanding the architecture of such a synagogue, Gamla is a must-see.

The parking lot is the starting point for a variety of hikes that vary in length, level of difficulty, and the experiences they offer. To get a taste of the volcanic plateau known in the Bible as Bashan or Gaulanitis (modern Golan Heights), consider a walk past the Gamla lookout on the trail to the Gamla waterfalls. In the winter and spring, this trail is filled with an evolving display of wildflowers. You may also catch a glimpse of the park's wildlife, which includes the wild boar, mountain gazelle, and rock hyrax. Don't forget to look up, because the reserve also plays host to local and migrant species of birds, including raptors. The most striking of these is the griffon vulture. These endangered raptors nest on the cliff faces in the reserve and soar on the thermals with a wingspan that can exceed eight feet. The trail to the falls also leads you back in time past a Byzantine village and a series of dolmens. A dolmen is a Middle Bronze tomb constructed with vertical and horizontal stone slabs. The body was placed in the window created by the slabs, and then the entire structure was covered with stones.

The national park also preserves the ancient Jewish village of Gamla, which you can see from the Gamla lookout. From here, a more rustic and steep trail descends toward the canyon floor and into the village ruins. As you carefully make your way down this trail, it is easy to see how the place received its name. *Gamla* is the Aramaic word for "camel." The village literally hangs off the side of a ridge that resembles the hump of a camel. While it is not mentioned in the Bible, this was a thriving village at the time of Jesus. During the First Jewish Revolt (beginning in AD 66), the citizens of Gamla enhanced the natural defenses of the village with walls and towers. These enhancements created a secure location to which many refugees and revolutionaries fled in the face of the advancing Roman army. By AD 67 the fight had come to Gamla. The Roman general Vespasian attacked the village, breeching the wall near the location at which the modern path enters the ruins. According to Josephus, as Roman soldiers charged through the village, four thousand Jews died in the streets while some five thousand leaped to their death from the summit. The fierceness of the fighting is attested archaeologically. Within the ruins, excavators found one thousand catapult stones and sixteen hundred arrowheads. Replicas of the Roman siege weapons that hurled such projectiles are present on the path leading to the village.

In more peaceful times the Jews of this village gathered in their synagogue. The foundations of this rectangular building have survived, giving you the chance to visit one of the oldest synagogues in Israel. It was built in the first century BC and functioned until the time of its destruction in AD 67. The steps around the walls of the synagogue were the seats for those who gathered to worship. The niche in the corner of the building held the holy scrolls. And the paving stones set in the floor mark the spot from which the Scriptures were read. While the Gospels do not record a visit of Jesus to Gamla, it is likely he made his way to this Jewish village and spoke in this building.

INFORMATION 📍 northeast of the Sea of Galilee along Route 808, fifty kilometers from Tiberias; 🔘

Har Bental (Mount Bental)

Har Bental (Mountain of the Son of the Dew) is one of many inactive cinder cones that once produced the lava flows, ejected basaltic boulders, and provided the dark soils of the Golan Heights. What makes this cone stand out is its elevation. At 3,842 feet, this mountain offers one of the most striking views in northern Israel. From here you have an unobstructed view of Mount Hermon, the Huleh Basin, and the Sea of Galilee, as well as a look deep into modern Syria. As you might expect, this high perch on the border between modern Israel and Syria has a military heritage evidenced by the abandoned bunkers, trenches, and silhouettes of soldiers on its summit. But this high perch also allows a look into Bible stories like Jesus's temptation on a "very high mountain," his transfiguration on that same mountain, and Saul's conversion on the road to Damascus.

Mount Hermon dominates the view to the north. This is the southernmost ridge of the Anti-Lebanon Mountains that rises dramatically above all its geographical competitors (9,232 feet). Annual precipitation on the summit approaches seventy inches, most in the form of snow. So deep into the summer months you are likely to see snowfields trailing down its flanks like fingers. Today Mount Hermon marks the border between the modern states of Israel, Syria, and Lebanon, each of which claims a piece of this mountain. While it functioned similarly as a landmark and border marker in Bible times (Josh. 13:5, 11), it was best known as a travel obstacle. Both merchants and soldiers of

Bible times were ill-equipped to navigate directly over Mount Hermon. Consequently, the International Highway connecting the promised land and Damascus (just thirty-seven miles away from Har Bental) traveled below the eastern and southern flanks of Mount Hermon.

The biblical authors knew this massive ridge as Mount Hermon, Mount Sirion, and Mount Senir. What characteristically stood out in the mind of the Old Testament writers was its persistent snow cover (Jer. 18:14), rich timber supply (Ezek. 27:5), large predators (Song 4:8), and plentiful dewfall (Ps. 133:3). While no specific events of importance are associated with Mount Hermon in the Old Testament, that changes dramatically in the New Testament. For Matthew, this is the "very high mountain" that hosted several episodes from Jesus's life. Satan took Jesus here and "showed him all the kingdoms of the world and their splendor." This is likely a representative "showing" accomplished by pointing Jesus to the wide array of merchants and goods traveling the road below them. Satan's goal was to offer Jesus a kingdom without the cross, an offer Jesus quickly refused (Matt. 4:8–10). Fittingly, Jesus uses the same setting to announce the start of his last trip to Jerusalem, declaring that he will bring in God's kingdom with his suffering and death (Matt. 16:13, 21). Knowing this plan would appear preposterous and knowing he would need the disciples' support, Jesus takes Peter, James, and John onto the flanks of this "high mountain" to validate the plan via his transfiguration (Matt. 17:1–8).

The book of Acts highlights one more critical event that occurred within view of your high perch. Look northeast in the direction of the distant quarry and you are looking at a segment of the International Highway that Christians remember as the road to Damascus. Along this road, Jesus met Saul (Paul) and initiated the conversion that began his career as the great missionary to the gentiles (Acts 9:1–22). This story intimately involves the travel limitations imposed by Mount Hermon. Jews in Mesopotamia who were on their way to Jerusalem for the high festivals traveled through Damascus. Jewish believers in Jesus who lived there used this opportunity to speak with these pilgrims about their faith in Jesus the Messiah. That is why Saul, armed with authority to arrest such missionaries, headed to Damascus. However, his plan to put a stop to it all was reversed by Jesus. The Lord appeared to Saul, challenged his assumptions, and then sent him on to Damascus. Once there, Saul began to do exactly what he had intended to stop others from doing. He used the transportation hub of Damascus at the base of Mount Hermon to speak convincingly about Jesus the Messiah to those traveling through Damascus on the International Highway.

INFORMATION south of Merom Golan on the road that travels south from Route 959;

Hazor

Tel Hazor National Park preserves the largest archaeological site in Israel. The ancient city of Hazor expanded and contracted many times between the third millennium BC, when it was founded, and 732 BC, when the Assyrians destroyed it. It occupied two hundred acres at its zenith (eighteenth to thirteenth century BC). During the latter part of this era, Joshua, Deborah, and Barak fought against this mighty city.

The size, wealth, and military prowess of ancient Hazor are all intimately connected to its location along the International Highway. From the parking lot, you can see the natural obstacles that lie to the west and to the east, which funneled ancient travelers past Hazor. To the west are the sharply rising mountains of Upper Galilee. To the east and northeast is the Huleh Basin. Today this basin is farmland, but prior to the 1950s this was a thirty-thousand-acre swamp. The only passable route for international travelers moving through the promised land lay between swamp and mountains. This meant they traveled right past Hazor. For centuries Hazor took advantage of this location, collecting tariffs from passing merchants. This generated the wealth that accounts for Hazor's remarkable size and for its advanced military technology, which included nine hundred iron-fitted chariots (Judg. 4:13).

Let's start with the archaeology directly linked to the culture of biblical Israel. From the parking area, walk to the footprint of the tenth-century-BC gatehouse. This six-chambered structure and the walls that run north and south from it secured the citadel of Solomon's Hazor (1 Kings 9:15). A casemate wall system extends from the gate. This method of building a wall went well beyond the simpler, single-wall barricade. A casemate wall consisted of two parallel walls, built just a few yards apart, whose gap was filled with rock and soil. This type of wall was easier and faster to build and provided more strength than a single-wall barrier.

Walk to the west side of the park and you will enter architecture that dates to the time of King Ahab's expansion of Hazor (ninth century BC). This expansion provided room for more people, but it also created the need for access to a secure water supply. So within the defensive walls of the city, ancient excavators dug a rectangular shaft 130 feet down to the water table. The modern set of stairs built next to the ancient stone steps allows you to do what the ancients did: use the ancient shaft to walk thirteen stories down to the water table. The water system entry is located just a few steps southwest of the Canaanite palace.

Before the Israelites were here, Hazor was a Canaanite city-state. You can visit the remains of its royal palace lying between the Israelite water system and the six-chambered gatehouse. The contents of this palace are so precious that a modern roof has been erected over it to aid in its preservation. As you walk past the massive entry columns into the throne room of the king, imagine that you are walking into the presence of the premiere leader of Canaan at the time of Joshua (Josh. 11:10). Then imagine the fire that destroyed this palace. In about 1250 BC a fire raged through this structure. Olive oil stored in the adjacent building provided additional fuel, allowing the temperature of the inferno to soar to 2,350°F. At this temperature the basalt building stones cracked, and the organic material consumed in the blaze left an ash layer three feet deep!

Who was responsible for this fire? The Egyptian and Canaanite images, mutilated by those responsible for the fire, rule them out as the likely aggressors. The only other people group in the area at this time were the Israelites, so it is assumed that they were responsible for the raging inferno. But which Israelites? We know that Joshua not only attacked but burned Hazor (Josh. 11:11). If Joshua led Israel into Canaan in the thirteenth century BC, then this could be evidence of that destruction. On the other hand, it is possible that this destruction dates to the time of Deborah and Barak. A rejuvenated Hazor had been oppressing Israel for twenty years (Judg. 4:1–3). In time the Lord used Deborah and Barak to provide a miraculous victory over Hazor that took place in the Jezreel Valley well to the southwest. The Bible does not report on what happened next. But if the Israelite army's advance continued to Hazor and they set the Canaanite royal palace ablaze as Joshua had done, then this fire damage could be connected with the time of the judges.

In both Bible stories about Hazor, there is something to appreciate here. The Bible lists many cities that the Israelites defeated. They all have the same appearance in print on the pages of our Bibles and even on the maps in the back of our Bibles, but Hazor was different. This large, technically advanced city was the best in the region, a symbol of power and strength. When the Lord crafted an Israelite victory over a city like this, it highlighted the power and capability of Israel's God. That is a lesson that puts historical meat on the bones of this powerful language: "God is our refuge and strength, an ever-present help in trouble" (Ps. 46:1).

INFORMATION 📍 take Highway 90 north from the Sea of Galilee until you reach the road leading to Ayelet HaShahar; the entry to the national park is off this road; 🅿️

Heptapegon (Tabgha)

Both the Greek and Aramaic names of this location allude to the "seven springs" that deposit their warm water into the Sea of Galilee here. Byzantine Christians built two churches along the shoreline to recall two separate events in Jesus's life: the feeding of the five thousand (Matt. 14:13–21; Mark 6:32–44; Luke 9:10–17; John 6:1–13) and the restoration of the disciples, including Peter, that followed a miraculous catch of fish (John 21:1–23).

Two modern buildings on this campus recall these events. The Church of the Multiplication of the Loaves and Fishes is the lighter-colored limestone building (1982) modeled on and built over an earlier Byzantine church. It is a traditional location that recalls the feeding of the five thousand. The current church preserves a number of colorful Byzantine mosaics, including the famous one of the basket of bread and fish located in front of the modern altar. Closer to the shoreline, a darker basalt chapel (1933) is also built over earlier Byzantine structures. This is the Church of the Primacy of Saint Peter, which recalls Jesus's restoration of Peter. For those in the Roman Catholic tradition, this marks the moment when Jesus elevated Peter to a position of leadership over the entire church.

You may find things to be a bit quieter along the lakeshore. The warm springs create an environment that attracts the lake's fish, making this a desirable fishing spot. That means it may well be the location both for Jesus's first call of the disciples with a miraculous catch of fish (Luke 5:1–11) and for his recalling of the disciples to service with the same miracle (John 21:1–14). The symmetry between these events, aided by the parallel geographical setting, is important to note. Jesus appears to the disciples to recall them to service following his resurrection in the same place he first called them at the start of his ministry. This includes Peter, who not only abandoned Jesus but verbally denied any form of connection to him. How comforting to note that despite their failure to fully understand all that Jesus had taught, and despite their abandonment of Jesus after his arrest, the disciples still had a valid call to serve. For those of us who have failed the Lord at any point in our lives, there is something powerful to reflect on here as well.

INFORMATION 📍 along Highway 87 just southwest of its junction with Highway 90, on the west shore of the Sea of Galilee; 🚫 🚶

Jezreel

The fortress that King Ahab built at Tel Jezreel played vital economic, military, and defensive roles for the northern kingdom he ruled. But it is the adjacent vineyard of Naboth the Jezreelite that becomes the focus of the Old Testament authors. Here Ahab, Jezebel, and their affinity for Baal met divine judgment.

King Ahab built a fortress here in the ninth century BC that functioned in three ways for his kingdom. The first was economic. Ahab planned to redirect trade off the King's Highway that had traveled east of the Jordan River valley so that it would move through his country en route to world markets accessed via Phoenicia to the north. The marriage of Ahab to the Phoenician princess Jezebel helped secure the international connections through her country. The location of Jezreel was part of this strategy because it lay along the transportation artery through which those redirected goods would move and because the local topography created a bottleneck, limiting travel options, making it an ideal tax-collection station.

Of course, this economic strategy put King Ahab at odds with the national interests of Aram, which would otherwise have collected taxes on the same goods as they moved through Damascus. A fight was inevitable, and that became the second reason for establishing a fortress at Jezreel. When it became necessary to fight Aram, Israelite soldiers could muster here prior to traveling east into the Transjordan for battles that were sure to follow. Ahab died in just such a battle with Aram at Ramoth Gilead in 853 BC (1 Kings 1:29–38).

If those battles did not go well and Aram counterattacked against Israel, Jezreel functioned in a third way for Ahab. Aramean soldiers advancing against Samaria, the capital of Israel, had to march right past Jezreel on their way to the Ridge Route that would take them south to the capital. The entry to the Ridge Route lies to your west in the mountainous terrain near the modern city of Jenin. Thus Jezreel served as an early warning station to announce an impending attack against Samaria.

Given the strategic role this small ridge could play in achieving his economic, military, and defensive goals, Ahab built a fortress here whose remains are still being uncovered by archaeologists. To date, they have found a twenty-foot-deep dry moat that surrounds a walled fortress with four defensive tours. The entire compound covers an area slightly more than ten acres in size. Little of this archaeological evidence will be intelligible to the average visitor at this stage of the site's development.

You will be better served by taking a short walk to a viewing platform where the local geography and the setting of stories surrounding Naboth's vineyard come into view. Follow the paved trail that leaves the parking lot. As you walk, you will pass a number of cisterns and winepress floors associated with vineyards that covered this slope. Within five minutes you will arrive at the partially covered observation platform. From here you are able to look west into the open and fertile Jezreel Valley, north toward Mount Moreh, east down the Harod Valley toward the Transjordan, and southeast toward Mount Gilboa. The spring of Jezreel that provided water for the ancient fortress still flows. It is located about two thousand feet to the northeast near the cluster of trees in the valley below. Naboth's vineyard was likely positioned on the slope between the fortress and the spring.

This vineyard and Jezreel itself are repeatedly mentioned in 1 and 2 Kings. It all starts when Ahab wanted to acquire the vineyard of Naboth the Jezreelite. Because this plot of ground was near the fortress, he wanted it for himself so that he could turn it into a vegetable garden. When Naboth refused, Jezebel invented charges and manipulated the judicial proceedings to bring about Naboth's execution. With that accomplished, Ahab and Jezebel seized the vineyard (1 Kings 21:1–28). This is a disturbing story that highlights royal arrogance and the abuse of royal power. But it also highlights the spiritual failings of Ahab. In Israel, land and religion were intimately bound. The land a family owned, including the vineyard of Naboth, provided spiritual assurance that the promises given to Abraham were moving toward their redemptive conclusion (Gen. 12:1–3). This was something for which the Baal-worshiping Ahab and Jezebel had no respect. Consequently, the Lord promised a response that involved the shedding of royal blood on the very plot of ground that Ahab and Jezebel stole from Naboth (1 Kings 21:17–19).

The Lord delivered that response some time later when Ahab's son, Joram, ruled Israel. The Lord had commissioned a senior army officer named Jehu to eradicate the worship of Baal from Israel and in the process the royal family who sponsored it (2 Kings 9:1–10). Jehu had been fighting Aram in the Transjordan, advancing the economic agenda we noted above. He boarded his chariot and drove with reckless abandoned down the Harod Valley toward you and the fortress of Jezreel. Joram rode out in his own chariot and met Jehu near Naboth's vineyard. He was quickly dispatched by an arrow to the heart. Then Jehu directed his chariot officer to throw Joram's body on the plot of ground that belonged to Naboth the Jezreelite (2 Kings 9:14–26).

But divine justice had one more unsettled account, the one with Jezebel. The queen mother watched all this from a window in the fortress above you. At Jehu's direction, she was hurled from the window and trampled to death under the hoofs of Jehu's horses. Jehu went into the fortress to eat. Afterward he directed that the remains of Jezebel be buried. But when his staff looked for her in the gate, most of her body was missing. Dogs had gotten to her first. They dragged her body off to Naboth's vineyard and were having a meal of their own on the very spot Elijah had promised justice would be served (2 Kings 9:30–36). This story of divine justice begins and ends in Naboth's vineyard, illustrating that although the mills of divine justice may grind slowly, they grind exceedingly fine.

> **INFORMATION** 📍 on the east side of the Jezreel Valley along Route 675, just east of its junction with Highway 60; 🚫

Katzrin Historic Village

Katzrin is a historic village established to assist those reading the traditional Jewish writings (particularly the Talmud of the fourth to eighth century AD). Because this literature frequently makes reference to ancient cultural practices and household tools, this restored village is used as a teaching tool for Jewish students. Because many of the same cultural artifacts and practices are also mentioned in the Bible, this village has something to offer Christian Bible readers as well.

A web of level paths winds through this restored farm village. Start your visit by walking to the overlook above the residential area. From here you can get a sense for the size of the village and the way it is laid out. Then move to the partially rebuilt home where the construction methods using the native basalt come to life. Next door is a fully reconstructed house, roof and all. Walking through this home will take you back in time and give you the feel of living within a New Testament–era house in northern Israel. Inside you will find a variety of household items, including an oven, hand mills for grinding grain, baskets for sifting grain, looms, storage jars, and furniture. Both inside this home and in adjacent areas you can see tools associated with agriculture, including a scratch plow, winnowing fork, threshing floor, and threshing sledge. Nearby is an olive processing area with both an olive crushing press and an olive beam press. Near the center of the village you will find a partially reconstructed sixth-century-AD synagogue.

INFORMATION

 in the modern city of Qatsrin along Road 9088;

This restored village highlights the great distance between our daily lives and the lives of people in Bible times. Because the Lord used the cultural experiences and tools of the biblical authors to convey his thoughts to us, everything we can do to more intimately connect to the culture of the biblical world will yield new insights for us as Bible readers.

Korazim National Park (Chorazin)

This ancient Jewish town resides on a hillside nine hundred feet above the Sea of Galilee with wonderful views of the northern lake basin. Its surviving ruins date from the third to fifth century AD but provide cultural insights into how people lived here during the first century when Jesus regularly visited this town.

This is the best place to see and understand how New Testament homes were built in the Sea of Galilee basin. It was always easiest to build with local stone, so here that meant building with basalt. This kind of stone with a volcanic past is harder to shape than limestone and tends to fracture if used to span more than a few feet. These limitations changed the way people built. Given the difficulty harvesting and shaping this stone, it was desirable to use less of it. As you walk through the excavation, note how these builders sought to conserve materials by constructing stone walls fashioned like a modern stud wall and by building with arches. Given this type of stone's inability to

An *insula* home complex. This artist's rendition shows three men lowering their friend to Jesus for healing.

span large openings, those building with it built rooms that were smaller and narrower. Small living spaces ran counter to the culture of the Israelites, who tended to live in large, extended-family compounds. The solution to this conflict between building-material limitations and cultural needs was to build according to an *insula* plan. As noted in the discussion of Capernaum, this label comes from the island-like courtyard in the center of the living compound that was surrounded by a sea of smaller rooms. To get a sense for it, look for the large cobbled courtyard centrally located in the park. The *insula* provided the open-air space shared by the extended family and used for many daily tasks. Around the perimeter of the courtyard, each nuclear family had its own smaller private room. This is the architectural setting for the household stories we read in the Gospels that occur in the Galilee lake basin. This includes Mark 2:1–12. Jesus was in Capernaum speaking in one of the small rooms like those you see here, with crowds filling and spilling out of the courtyard, trying to hear what he was saying. Unable to penetrate the crowd, the friends of a disabled man hoisted him to the roof and brought him to Jesus by tearing a hole in the organic material that made up the roof.

To the west of this central courtyard is where you will find a partially reconstructed fourth-century-AD synagogue. It is distinguished by its size (fifty feet by seventy feet) and three large doorways facing Jerusalem. Within the synagogue, archaeologists uncovered a special seat dubbed the "seat of Moses." (The original is in the Israel Museum, but a replica remains on-site.) This was the seat from which the authorized teacher would interpret and apply the day's Scripture reading. Jesus made mention of it, urging his followers to listen to teachers of the law and the Pharisees who "sit in Moses' seat" but not to emulate their actions, which were less noble than their words (Matt. 23:2–3).

Although Jesus appears to have spent considerable time in Chorazin, the Gospels mention no specific event from his ministry here. However, Jesus made it clear that Chorazin, together with Bethsaida and Capernaum, benefited from his ministry by seeing him more often than did other towns and villages in Galilee. Connect these three towns and villages with a line on a map, and you have defined what some have called the evangelical triangle—this geographical triangle formed by Chorazin, Bethsaida, and Capernaum defines the space in which Jesus conducted the bulk of his Galilean ministry. He likely chose this area because of its proximity to the International Highway, allowing news of what he said and did to travel well beyond this small triangle of towns. But the special opportunity Chorazin enjoyed was squandered. In a sharply worded rebuke lamenting the opportunity lost (Matt. 11:20–24; Luke 10:13–15), Jesus gives each of us something to think about too. Have I failed to fully appreciate and respond to the opportunities that the Lord has given to me?

> **INFORMATION**
>
> 📍 east of modern Chorazim along Road 8277; 🚗

Kursi National Park

When Jesus told the disciples to get into a boat so that they could travel with him to the "other side" of the Sea of Galilee (Luke 8:22), they were not just changing geographical locations. This meant traveling to a completely different cultural setting. At the time of Jesus, the northwest side of the lake had an observant Jewish culture; the east side of the lake was gentile. This is the region of the Gerasenes and the Decapolis in which Jesus performed two striking miracles: an exorcism that resulted in evil spirits being cast into pigs (Luke 8:26–39) and the miraculous feeding of four thousand households (Mark 8:1–10). Kursi National Park provides a location to reflect on both.

The size of the monastery complex built here by European Christians in the fifth century indicates just how highly they regarded this spot. A wall surrounds an area 476 feet by 404 feet. Within the wall you can see the partially restored church and its surviving mosaic floors. The path and stairway that climbs the ridge to the south of the church will lead you to a smaller Byzantine chapel. This marks the traditional location of the cave in which lived the demon-possessed man whom Jesus healed.

What motivated this kind of building in a place that today gets very little attention? These European Christians came here to reflect on two stories that showed Jesus's great love and concern for gentiles like them. Jesus left the northwest side of the lake predominated by an observant Jewish population and traveled to this gentile area in order to heal a man who lived in a place that was as non-Jewish as you could imagine. It was under the control of Hippos (just to the south of Kursi), a Decapolis city designed to communicate the ideology and spiritual values of the Greco-Roman world to the locals. In short, it was a place where the locals raised pigs. The demon-possessed man Jesus healed here was a gentile. After his healing, this gentile man wanted to follow Jesus to the Jewish side of the lake. But Jesus said to him, "Return home and tell how much God has done for you" (Luke 8:39). He did. And later when Jesus returned to the Decapolis (Mark 7:31), four thousand households abandoned their daily routines to hear him teach. They became so intent on being with Jesus that they had not taken care to bring food to the remote location. In fact, they showed no concern for food even when wracked by hunger pangs. This is when Jesus addressed their need by miraculously providing a meal for the four thousand. It is no wonder that gentile Christians came to love this side of the lake.

And they still do, particularly when they think about the larger theological message taught by the feeding of the five thousand and the feeding of the four thousand. Jesus performed these near-identical miracles in two different locations for two different ethnic groups. Later he used these two events and their geographical backstory to address a mistaken impression being communicated by some Jewish teachers of his day. They taught that gentiles had either an inferior role to play in the kingdom of God or no role at all. Jesus used these two feeding miracles to correct this mistaken impression (Matt. 16:5–12). He fed five thousand households on the observant Jewish side of the lake, and he fed four thousand households on the gentile, eastern side of the lake. While these two miracles addressed the hunger of his students, they also demonstrated that Jesus did not make a distinction between Jewish and gentile students. Both were fit for the kingdom. Jesus was and is the Savior for all people no matter where they live or what their ethnic heritage may be.

INFORMATION 📍 five and a half kilometers north of Ein Gev along Highway 92; 🚗

⭐ Megiddo

Megiddo is one of the most strategic locations in the ancient world. Caravans and armies traveled through Israel because it provided a land bridge between the continents of Asia, Africa, and Europe. In doing so, they traveled right past Megiddo, which in turn played a more prominent role in the ancient Near Eastern world than its fifteen-acre size might suggest. This critically located city slipped in and out of Israel's hands just as it slips on and off the pages of the Bible. King Josiah died in battle near Megiddo (2 Kings 23:29). And the apostle John links the final days of world history to this place (Rev. 16:16). In Hebrew, Armageddon means "hill of Megiddo."

Stories of Megiddo are intimately linked to geography. The sprawling Jezreel Valley, which lies to the east of Megiddo, provided the easiest east–west passage through the central mountains of the promised land. But to get to this valley from the coastal plain, it was necessary to get past the brush-filled ridges of Mount Carmel. The best route through this natural roadblock was the Megiddo Pass (also called the Arunah Pass or Iron Pass). Here softer limestone eroded to create a natural passageway. Near Megiddo the passageway narrowed to an opening best measured in feet rather than miles. (It has been widened significantly and carries the modern Highway 65.) With travel options severely limited by the terrain, this was the ideal place to collect trade revenue and to control the movement of armies. When the empire-building Egyptian Thutmose III contemplated its value, he gave Megiddo this sterling compliment: "To capture Megiddo is to capture a thousand towns."

After you have walked through the visitor center / museum, the modern path will lead you to the ancient gates of Megiddo. The first is a sixteenth-century-BC ceremonial gatehouse (built at the close of Israel's stay in Egypt) that provided entry into a Canaanite palace. Note the U-shaped channels cut into the walls of this structure, which held wood beams. This building style (alluded to in 1 Kings 6:36 and Ezra 6:4) added a flexible component to the otherwise rigid stone structure. During an earthquake the wood beams would dampen the seismic waves, improving the building's chances for survival. The second gatehouse dates to the time of Solomon (1 Kings 9:15). By this time the earlier gatehouse had been buried, so Solomon built his gatehouse over the top of this structure. You can see the remains of Solomon's massive entry to Megiddo after walking up the modern set of stairs that lie just inside the earlier gatehouse. To get the best sense of how this gate complex looked in the tenth century BC, check out the model in the park's museum.

Continue walking to the east side of the archaeological site. From here you will get stunning views of the Jezreel Valley and the best view of the Canaanite temple precinct located in the trench below you. Your eyes are sure to catch, among the foundations of rectangular temples from various ages, the unique round altar (twenty-five feet in diameter and four and a half feet tall) accessed by a set of stairs. This Canaanite altar dates to approximately 2700 BC, built some six hundred years before Abram entered this land.

Retrace your steps and watch for the pathway that leads toward the south side of the excavation where the remains of three installations provide insights into life in ancient Megiddo. The first is a round pit lined with fieldstones (thirty-six feet in diameter and twenty-three feet deep). Two sets of ancient stairs, which can still be seen on the perimeter of the pit, provided access to its contents. This is an underground grain silo with the capacity to hold one thousand tons of wheat. Its wheat may have been used to feed the chariot horses, whose stables are located just to the south of the silo. One of these buildings has been partially restored so you can see how they would have looked. The stables were long buildings with three aisles. The open central aisle created access to the two side aisles where the animals were kept. Between the pillars that line the central aisle, you can see stone mangers used to feed the animals. Just west of these buildings is a water system from the ninth century BC. So that residents could access water without exiting the security of the walled city, a 115-foot shaft was dug down to a 210-foot horizontal passage to a spring. You can walk through this system to the spring and back using the modern set of 183 stairs.

With a better understanding of Megiddo in hand, it is time to open your Bible. Let's start with 2 Chronicles 35:20–24, which reports the untimely death of King Josiah. This godly Israelite king mistakenly believed that the Lord wanted him to stop the large Egyptian army poised to march through the Megiddo Pass en route to a major battle at Carchemish, on the Euphrates River. Egypt did not want a fight with Josiah. They were on their way to assist the waning Assyrian army in a battle that would occur far from the land ruled by Josiah. But given all the past harm that Assyria had done to God's chosen people, Josiah was not kindly disposed to this Egyptian plan. He was determined to stop Egypt's advance.

But why take on the Egyptian army here? Topography certainly played a role in Josiah's decision. The narrow opening of the pass just west of Megiddo is the one place where a smaller Israelite army had a chance against the larger army of Egypt. Rather than fighting the whole Egyptian army at once, Israel had to fight only the soldiers who exited the restricted opening in the pass. But there is more to Josiah's choice of Megiddo than military tactics. Ironically, the Bible stories that played out in view of Megiddo may also have had a role in his decision to fight Egypt here. Megiddo overlooks a geographical area in which the Lord had frequently provided unexpected victories for those faithful to him. Elijah defeated the 450 prophets of Baal on Mount Carmel (1 Kings 18), Israelite infantry defeated a Canaanite chariot corps in the valley in front of Megiddo at the time of Deborah and Barak (Judg. 4–5), and the outnumbered Gideon defeated Midianites just north of Mount Moreh (Judg. 7). Given how the Lord had granted improbable victories here, Josiah may well have thought he was next on the list. He was wrong. Josiah was shot by Egyptian archers and died soon after.

But Revelation 16:16 mentions another battle in which the Lord will provide not just certain but also ultimate victory. John tells us that "the kings of the world" who oppose the Lord will gather their forces for war at "Armageddon." Whether this language is meant to identify the location of a real battle or is being used figuratively for a Megiddo-like battle is debated. But the defeat of all paganism at the end of time is as certain as what is to follow: the Lamb will sit on his throne and rule a sin-free, eternal kingdom (Rev. 21–22).

> **INFORMATION** 📍 just north of the Highway 66/65 intersection and adjacent to the Jezreel Valley; 🚗

✪ Mount Arbel National Park and Nature Reserve

When you grow weary of the crowded sites along the shoreline of the Sea of Galilee and need a quiet place to reflect that includes an absolutely stunning view, Mount Arbel is your spot. This park preserves a worthy corner of Israel's natural world that includes two sharply defined cliff faces, the deep valley between them, and an array of plants and animals. What is more, Mount Arbel is the most likely setting for the Sermon on the Mount (Matt. 5–7) and the Great Commission (Matt. 28:16–20).

The national park offers walks of varying length and difficulty, some of which include climbing on the vertical cliff faces using a variety of climbing aids anchored to the rock. No matter how much adventure you would like to weave into this visit, be sure to include the walk from the visitor center to the Carob and Kinneret Lookouts. Within twenty minutes of walking, this easy path will bring you to the top of Mount Arbel, where you will enjoy an unobstructed view 1,280 feet above the Sea of Galilee. This view is a treasure not to be missed. To the southwest your eyes will catch the top of the dome-shaped Mount Tabor, which rises above the Jezreel Valley. To the west is an extinct volcano. The small horn-like projections on either side of an otherwise flat summit give it its name, the Horns of Hittim. The higher mountains to the northwest are those of Upper Galilee. The opposing cliff face is Mount Nitay, part of the nature reserve, as is the valley between the cliffs, called the Wadi Hamam (Valley of the Doves). This sloping valley carried the International Highway down to the lake basin. The Plain of Gennesaret on the northwest shore stretches out before you in the direction of places like Capernaum, Korazim, and Bethsaida that witnessed the bulk of Jesus's Galilean ministry efforts.

Although Mount Arbel is not mentioned by name in the Gospels, it is the most likely setting for two important events: the Sermon on the Mount and the Great Commission. While most visitors will go to the traditional location associated with Jesus's giving of the Sermon on the Mount, the Mount of Beatitudes, Mount Arbel is a more likely setting for several reasons. The advanced instruction Jesus was giving his disciples required some privacy available here but not on the busy lakeshore. What is more, this location fits the contrasting geographic descriptions of the Sermon on the Mount given in Matthew and Luke. Mount Arbel with its plateau-like summit and stunning cliff faces is simultaneously a mountain and a level place (Matt. 5:1; Luke 6:17). The summit of Mount Arbel with its horizon-to-horizon view also invites the kind of personal reflection that is expressed in the content of the Sermon on the Mount. This is particularly true of the Beatitudes (Matt. 5:1–12). As Jesus surveyed the various seasons of the human experience, he invited the disciples to contemplate the difference between the reality mortals see and the one God sees. The poor are really rich. Those who mourn will find comfort. And those who show mercy and seek peace will in turn be blessed. These words stimulate thought wherever they are spoken. But here on the summit of Mount Arbel, the disciples were actually looking down into the lives of ordinary people in the plain below, just as God does. Rather than merely inviting them to imagine the human realities surveyed in the Beatitudes, Jesus was inviting the disciples to look into the very lives of people among whom they had walked.

As Jesus went on, the view from this summit continued to contribute to the message. Urging the disciples to be salt and a lighted city on a hill (Matt. 5:13–16), Jesus had two locations in view. Magdala, at the base of Mount Arbel, was where salt was used to preserve fish caught on the Sea of Galilee. Hippos, a Decapolis city on the opposite shore, was a city designed to sell the Greco-Roman worldview to the locals, in part through the lights that illuminated it at night. As Jesus urged the disciples to become like salt and an illuminated city set on a hill, his message was clearer and more memorable because it was attached to real places the disciples could see. And when worry stirred in their hearts over this assignment or life's challenges in general, Jesus invited them to look around at the flowers and birds, still very much a part of this nature reserve. Why worry? As the heavenly Father sees to the basic needs of the flora and fauna, so he will attentively meet every need of his children (Matt. 6:25–34).

The advanced theological education Jesus offered the disciples in the Sermon on the Mount is mirrored by another trip to a mountain in Galilee after his resurrection. Here Jesus would deliver his final words of encouragement and instruction to the disciples. Following Jesus's resurrection, the disciples were told that Jesus would meet them in Galilee (Matt. 28:7, 10). Apparently those instructions went so far as to include the very mountain on which they were to meet (Matt. 28:16). Although the specific mountain is not named in Matthew, Mount Arbel seems to be the most likely candidate. It is the one piece of rising terrain in the lake basin that is worthy of the distinctive label "mountain." What is more, the disciples had met with Jesus here before; it was the memorable location of their advanced instruction. Now Jesus had one more thing to say, the conclusion to his earlier instructions given during the Sermon on the Mount. Here, with a view that stretches to the horizon and overlooked the international caravans moving on the highway beneath them, Jesus urged them to take all they had seen and heard to people who lived throughout the world. His impassioned plea still resonates with this view: "Go and make disciples of all nations" (Matt. 28:19).

INFORMATION 📍 northwest of Tiberias; take Highway 77 to Road 7717; 🚗

Mount of the Beatitudes

Manicured lawns and beautiful gardens mark the traditional location for the Sermon on the Mount (Matt. 5–7), which begins with the recitation of the Beatitudes (Matt. 5:3–10).

A few unimpressive remains from the fourth century AD recall the era when Byzantine Christians came to this spot to reflect on the detailed manifesto in which Jesus provided insight and instruction for the church. Today Christian pilgrims gather around the modern chapel (1938) whose architecture and design seek to capture the content and spirit of Jesus's message. The chapel has eight sides, each with a stained-glass window dedicated to one of the Beatitudes presented in Latin. The floor of the chapel around the altar features the seven virtues championed throughout the Sermon on the Mount (justice, charity, prudence, faith, fortitude, hope, and temperance).

Although I prefer Mount Arbel as the location for the Sermon on the Mount (see above), the views from this hill, the solitude, and the longtime connection to the Sermon on the Mount create a wonderful place to reflect on its message, particularly the Beatitudes. Psalm 1 speaks of how blessed believers are. In the Beatitudes, Jesus takes us a step further. He reminds us that we live in a state of blessing even when life's circumstances suggest otherwise.

⭐ Mount Precipice (Nazareth)

Mount Precipice offers an excellent view into Nazareth and an outstanding panorama of the Jezreel Valley. It is widely regarded as one of the best views in Israel at sunset. But it was not the view that brought an angry Nazareth mob to the brow of this hill with Jesus in tow. They came to throw him off, intending to execute him because he had promoted an idea in their synagogue that they believed to be blasphemy (Luke 4:28–30).

As you take the short five-minute walk from the parking area to the viewpoint, look over your right shoulder to get an aerial view of modern Nazareth. From this vantage point, you can best capture the geographical realities of Jesus's home and the way geography shaped its culture. To get an idea of the size of the village Jesus knew, look for the Basilica of the Annunciation in the bottom of the valley. Most of first-century-AD Nazareth fit within this church compound. The home of Mary, Joseph, and Jesus was small, rural, and geographically isolated. It was nestled into the bottom of a valley that itself was inset into the top of a ridge. No one expected much from the place, as suggested by the words of Nathanael, "Nazareth! Can anything good come from there?" (John 1:46). We celebrate Nazareth as Jesus's longtime home, but he constantly battled the low expectations associated with the label "Jesus of Nazareth."

The view from the summit is breathtaking as well as educational. Certainly Jesus's parents would have taken him to this very spot to teach him the history of his people. The dome-shaped Mount Tabor to the east is linked to the story of Deborah and Barak (Judg. 4–5).

Mount Moreh to the southeast is linked with the story of Gideon (Judg. 7). Beyond Mount Moreh is Mount Gilboa, where King Saul's life ended (1 Sam. 31). Megiddo witnessed the death of King Josiah (2 Kings 23:29). And Mount Carmel to the west hosted the story of Elijah and the prophets of Baal (1 Kings 18:16–46). Jesus would have learned much from this view, but he also left his own mark here. When a widow tragically lost her only son, Jesus raised him from the dead. This happened in the village of Nain on the lower slopes of Mount Moreh in front of you (Luke 7:11–17). This miracle is a geographical partner to the one Elisha did on the opposite side of the same mountain in the village of Shunem (2 Kings 4:8–37). Jesus had another lesson to teach here. Just before the angry crowd attempted to use this ridge to kill him, he made an observation that may be the greatest tragedy of Nazareth: "No prophet is accepted in his hometown" (Luke 4:24).

INFORMATION 📍 travel south from Nazareth on Highway 60 for approximately half a kilometer after the main traffic circle; follow the signs and the winding road to the summit of Mount Kedumim; 🚫

Mukhraqa Monastery on Mount Carmel

The Arabic name al-Mukhraqa means "the sacrifice." The sword-wielding statue in the courtyard clarifies which sacrifice is remembered here. Elijah challenged the prophets of Baal to a contest involving a sacrifice on Mount Carmel (1 Kings 18:16–46). In the twelfth century AD, the Crusaders believed this to be the site of that contest. That led them to form the Carmelite religious order here and to found this monastery.

Begin your visit on the roof of the monastery, accessed via the stairs in the gift shop. At nearly sixteen hundred feet above sea level, the roof offers a commanding view of the region. From here you can see that Mount Carmel is actually an extended ridge, thirty miles long and up to twelve miles wide. Given the elevation and proximity of this ridge to the Mediterranean Sea, you can appreciate why Mount Carmel is a rain- and dew-rich environment. It receives considerably more annual moisture than the surrounding area, assuring that its slopes will be thick with vegetation even when the land around it becomes dry (Song 7:5; Isa. 35:2; Jer. 50:19; Amos 1:2). To the south you will see one of the softer limestone valleys that has eroded into a natural transportation route between the Jezreel Valley and the coastal plain. This is Jokneam Pass, which enters the Jezreel Valley below you at the modern city of Yokneam. On a clear day, the unobstructed view of the Jezreel Valley to the north and east is breathtaking and allows you to glimpse a number of locations important to Bible readers. To this end, use the location finder on the observation deck. It will help you to identify Nazareth, Mount Tabor, Mount Moreh, and Mount Gilboa.

The chapel and grounds offer a quiet place to walk and reflect on the great contest that occurred near here. Although the first of the Ten Commandments demands sole allegiance to the Lord, Ahab and Jezebel encouraged their subjects to worship Baal. They built a temple for Baal in their capital city and put Baal prophets on the state's payroll (1 Kings 16:32; 18:19). They believed that Baal provided the rain and dewfall. This public policy contradicted the clear word from the Lord, who said he provided this life-giving moisture (Deut. 8:10–14). The contest on Mount Carmel would resolve the tension between this claim and counterclaim. Needless to say, things had not been going well for Baal. When so many in Israel looked to Baal for water, the Lord turned it off, initiating a three-year famine (1 Kings 17:1; 18:1). The stress imposed on Israel's subjects by this famine set up the challenge issued by Elijah. Both he and prophets of Baal built an altar and prepared a sacrifice but did not ignite the wood piled beneath it.

Each was to call on their god, and the authentic deity would respond by spontaneously igniting the tinder.

The importance of the setting for the contest is underscored by its repeated mention within the story (1 Kings 18:19, 20, 42). To understand why, realize that many ancients believed deities performed more reliably in certain geographic locations than others (1 Kings 20:28). What is unreported in the Bible story, but well known beyond it, is that this rain- and dew-rich mountain was a Baal worship site. This is alluded to in a ninth-century-BC Assyrian reference to Mount Carmel that describes it as "Baal of the headlands." Think of what that means. When Elijah selected the location for the contest, he had selected a location at which Baal was expected to perform at his peak. Elijah gave home-field advantage to his opponents. But it also meant that if Baal failed here, his failure would be amplified by losing on his home turf. As the contest continued, it was the Lord, not Baal, who provided fire from heaven. The Lord's unmistakable response coupled with its location revealed Baal as a fraud who had no right to compete for Israel's allegiance or worship.

INFORMATION 📍 on Mount Carmel southeast of Daliyat el-Karmel; drive east from the Ha-Mukhraqa junction (located along Route 672) to reach the monastery entrance; 🚻 🅿️

Mount Tabor

This dome-shaped mountain rises abruptly from the northeast bay of the Jezreel Valley. Its distinct profile, elevation (1,929 feet), and isolation make it stand out particularly as you drive on Highway 60 toward Nazareth or Highway 65, which travels east of Tabor and climbs the natural ramp leading from the Jezreel Valley into the mountains of Lower Galilee (the same natural feature used by the ancient

International Highway). No matter if you drive by or stop for a visit on the summit, there are important Bible stories to consider here.

For Christians of the Byzantine and Crusader eras, Mount Tabor became the "high mountain" of Jesus's transfiguration (Matt. 17:1). This traditional memory led them to construct buildings on the summit whose remains are incorporated into the Latin Basilica of the Transfiguration (1924). To visit the church, follow the summit road up the mountain and through the thirteenth-century-AD Gate of the Wind.

While the authentic location for the transfiguration is Mount Hermon (see above), you may wish to make the drive up Mount Tabor for the view. Some will prefer the balcony of the Franciscan hospice at the summit, while others will opt for the viewpoint from the ridge about halfway up the mountain, a site favored by hang gliders. In either case, the panorama invites reflection on the story of Deborah and Barak (Judg. 4–5). During these leaders' lives, God's people again adopted the views of their pagan neighbors. So once again the Lord allowed Israel to be oppressed, this time by the wealthy city-state of Hazor and its fleet of nine hundred iron-fitted chariots. The chariots established a battle line in the Jezreel Valley near Megiddo, the very terrain on which they performed at their peak. The Israelites had no chariots, so their infantry gathered on Mount Tabor, terrain that favored them. The battle would not commence until one of the two left the terrain that favored their style of fighting. That happened when the Lord called for Barak and his soldiers to abandon the high ground and charge the chariots in the valley (Judg. 4:14–15). When Israel responded in faith to this divine command, the Lord rewarded their trust with an overwhelming victory that involved a sudden and unexpected rainstorm. Most of the Jezreel Valley drains to the northwest out the small gap in the terrain known as the Kishon Pass. When the valley receives too much rainfall in too little time, the valley floods. That is exactly what happened that day (Judg. 5:4, 21). The chariots, bogged down in the mud, became a hindrance rather than an advantage on the battlefield that now favored the Israelite infantry. The Israelites' experience affirms what we see so often in Scripture: trust in the Lord, even in the face of seemingly impossible odds, has its reward.

INFORMATION 📍 for the view from the summit, take Road 7266 on the north side of the mountain; 🚫 ⛰️

✪ Nazareth

Nazareth was the hometown of Mary and Joseph, the very place they encountered angelic messengers who told them that they were to be the parents of Jesus (Matt. 1:18–25; Luke 1:26–38). And it was this modest village that watched Jesus play, mature, and learn a trade, because he remained here until the age of thirty (Luke 2:39–40).

It is safe to say that Mary and Joseph would not recognize the place today. Their Nazareth was a small village nestled into the bottom of a valley, surrounded by higher ridges. By contrast, modern Nazareth fills the valley and spills over those ridges, seeking space to accommodate a population approaching one hundred thousand. The narrow streets that easily accommodated the locals now struggle to carry the burden of locals and tourists, all of whom seem to believe that honking their car horns will get them to their destinations faster. The quiet, rustic, four-acre Nazareth of Mary and Joseph is no more. Nevertheless, it is a must-stop for Christians who want see the place that so powerfully influenced Jesus and shaped others' perception of him, those who knew him as Jesus of Nazareth.

Modern Nazareth has many churches and many traditional stories associated with those churches that seek to fill in the gap left in the storytelling of the Gospels. You can visit the Church of Saint Gabriel, which is built over the village well believed by some to be the place

Gabriel visited Mary, and the Church of Joseph, which supposedly contains Joseph's workshop where both he and Jesus worked. Here we will focus on the Basilica of the Annunciation, because it is the largest and historically the most well documented of the lot. While not always easy to reach, it is easy to find. This is the largest of the churches in Nazareth.

From the fourth to the eighth century, Christian pilgrims mention seeing the house in which the angel Gabriel visited Mary or one of the churches built over the home. The modern basilica, completed in 1969, stands on the foundation a twelfth-century Crusader church, which in turn contains evidence of an earlier Byzantine church as well as an even earlier synagogue presumed to be a Jewish-Christian house of worship. To put first-century Nazareth in scale, realize that most of it lies beneath the footprint of this church compound. If you would like to visit the modest remains of the first-century homes, you can arrange for a guided tour that will take you under the church and into the accompanying museum. But most will opt for a visit to the church proper.

To enter the basilica, look for the main entry on the west side of the building. The large entry that greets you is filled with images of Old Testament stories that anticipate the coming of Jesus, while the artwork on the bronze doors points to key moments in Jesus's life. This entry leads to the lower floor of the basilica, which is simply decorated, dimly lit, and austere in feel. The design is meant to highlight the humanity of Jesus. The focal point of the lower floor is the small stone recess thought to be part of Mary's home and the place where she received news of Jesus's upcoming birth from Gabriel (Luke 1:26–38). This is where the few remains of the Byzantine and Crusader churches can be seen. The feel of the building changes dramatically when you walk upstairs. This part of the basilica is ornately decorated, colorful, and brightly lit, thanks to a cupola that soars 170 feet above you. It is all meant to remind us of the divinity of Jesus. Among the artwork on this floor, you will see a variety of pieces that depict Mary and the infant Jesus donated by Christians from throughout the world.

When you walk outside into the courtyard, look for a quiet place to reflect on the role of Mary and Joseph in caring for Jesus in Nazareth (Matt. 1:18–25; Luke 1:26–38). We often underestimate the faith and courage it took for them to execute the roles they played. They were both less than twenty years of age, Mary perhaps as young as thirteen when Gabriel visited her. Consider carefully what God was asking them to believe and do. God's people of the past had been waiting nearly 2,100 years, since the time of Abraham, for the birth of this special child. Who would have expected that a young, engaged couple from the backwater village of Nazareth would be the ones to bring the Messiah into the world? Certainly Mary and Joseph had not seen it coming. They were excited about their coming marriage. That is when God turned their world upside down. The angel tells Mary that she is going to become pregnant "through the Holy Spirit" so that her child will be the "Son of God" and not the biological son of Joseph. And yet Joseph was not to stop the marriage with a divorce but to take this child as his own. By doing so, Jesus became a descendant of David who would receive the "throne of his father David." While an angel delivered this message to both Mary and Joseph, they were left to explain it to their family and friends in this conservative Jewish village where shame was collectively shared by extended families. It is unimaginable that this news would have been warmly received in a place that already struggled with low self-image (John 1:46).

In your mind, take away the traffic, the crowds, and the vendors. Consider what it was like for Mary and Joseph. For them this was a hard story to believe, a hard story to tell, and a hard story to live. But they never missed a beat. They raised Jesus, protected him, and taught him the Scriptures, all the while deflecting the knowing looks and biting comments of family and friends. We owe them a debt of thanks for showing the remarkable character, strength, and maturity of faith that made it all possible.

INFORMATION 📍 Nazareth is most easily reached from the Jezreel Valley by using Highway 60; it is twelve kilometers north of Afula; the Basilica of the Annunciation is on Al-Bishara Street, in the heart of modern Nazareth;  🚫 🔺

Sea of Galilee

This inland lake goes by a variety of names, including Kinneret (given its harp-like shape), Lake of Tiberias, and Lake of Gennesaret. It is much smaller than most people expect, just seven and a half miles long and thirteen miles wide at its widest part. It has thirty-two miles of shoreline and

> A **cast net** was a hand-thrown net used to fish the shallow water near shore.

A **drag net** was rectangular in shape and was deployed by the combined efforts of a crew in a boat and on shore.

is approximately 155 feet deep. The lake sits in a deep basin (seven hundred feet below sea level) with higher terrain rising on all sides except the south, where we find the outlet for the lower Jordan River.

The Sea of Galilee that you see today is quite different than the lake of Jesus's time in two ways, both the product of modern changes to the ecosystem. You may notice that it is cloudy in appearance. This is due to the draining of the Huleh Basin, which lies just north of the Sea of Galilee. This basin had been a thirty-thousand-acre swamp that naturally filtered the waters of the upper Jordan River as they made their way into the Sea of Galilee. It was drained in the 1950s to create thirty thousand acres of arable farmland. Although the area now provides a tremendous amount of food, it no longer provides the natural filtration for the water that enters the lake basin. This has resulted in more turbid water and changes in the aquatic life of the lake.

The second change can clearly be seen on the south side of the lake where a dam has been installed. The modern state of Israel carefully manages water throughout the country. In part, that has been accomplished by placing a check dam at the south end of the Sea of Galilee so that its water level can be controlled. A small amount of water always passes through the dam so that a semblance of the lower Jordan River remains. But the natural lake is no more; it is a managed reservoir used to supply a portion of the country's water.

Despite these changes, the Sea of Galilee remains a beautiful place whose shoreline and surface are intimately linked to Jesus's mission on earth. On the lake itself, Jesus showed his unique nature by providing miraculous catches of fish and stilling storms (Matt. 8:23–27; 14:22–33; Mark 4:35–41; 6:45–56; Luke 5:1–11; 8:22–25; John 6:16–21; 21:1–13).

A **trammel net** was a multi-layer net designed for fishing the deep waters of the lake.

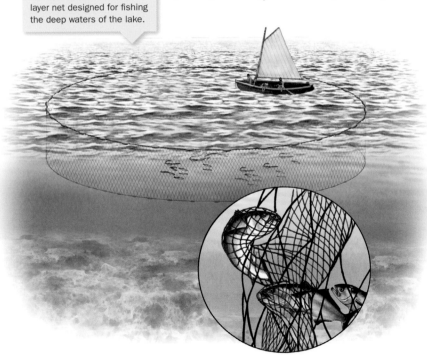

A **trammel boat** is the kind of boat used by the disciples for fishing on the Sea of Galilee.

INFORMATION 📍 the Sea of Galilee can be reached from Jerusalem by traveling east on Highway 1 and north on Highway 90, which will take you up the Jordan River valley; if you prefer the slower trip through the central mountains, travel north on Highway 60 from Jerusalem and then take Highway 65 and Highway 77 to the lake; 🚫

Sepphoris (Zippori National Park)

Although Sepphoris is not mentioned in the Bible, it was one of two major cities of Galilee in the first century AD. It is best known for the views it offers and its collection of ancient mosaics.

Located on a low rise north of the Nazareth Ridge and above the spacious Beit Netofa Valley, Sepphoris served as Herod Antipas's regional capital until about AD 20, when that honor shifted to the newly built city of Tiberias. By AD 200 the name of the place had changed to Zippori. That is when Jewish scholars gathered here to edit and preserve in writing the traditional teachings that became known as the Mishnah.

Walk from the parking lot toward the highest elevation in the park, marked by a sole building. This is the Crusader citadel. From the citadel's roof, the geography of Lower Galilee and its advantages will become clear. This region is marked by a series of east–west valleys separated from one another by east–west ridges. To the south you can see the southernmost of those ridges, the Nazareth Ridge. And to the north you can see the topographical pattern repeating with the Turan Valley, Turan Ridge, Beit Netofa Valley, and Jotapata Ridge. As you move north, each succeeding ridge gets a little higher. That means traveling north is like ascending a set of stairs that leads to the inaccessible and higher mountains of Upper Galilee. From this view, it is apparent that Lower Galilee offers wonderful farmland in the valleys. But it is the ridges that reorient the flow of traffic. North–south traffic moved to the edges of this region that favored east–west travel.

Mosaics are the other big draw of Sepphoris. They can be seen in the sidewalks of the two main streets (*cardo* and *decumanus*) and in the sixth- to seventh-century synagogue (northeast of the Crusader citadel, beyond and below the Roman theater). But the two most unique mosaics are located east of the citadel. The first is in the Roman villa (third century AD). Here 1.5 million tesserae (of twenty-three colors) are used to create a floor mosaic used as a dining table around which guests would recline to eat. The second is in the Nile House (sixth century AD). Here you will find a number of mosaics; the most striking is the floor design that seeks to capture the idea of prosperity using Egyptian symbolism.

Although there are few first-century remains here, Sepphoris is a good place to reflect on the differences between the culture of Judea to the south and the culture of Galilee to the north in Jesus's day. Herod built Sepphoris the way he did in order to combat some of the negative impressions that clung to the Galilee area. From a Judean perspective, Galileans were more rural, simple, imprecise with their language, and less cautious about preserving their Jewish identity. This perception rubbed off even on a local like Nathanael, who was from Cana of Galilee. He questioned if anything of value could come from the region and Nazareth in particular (John 1:46).

Perhaps that is why Jesus did his first miracle in the little village of Cana (north of Sepphoris on the south side of the Beit Netofa Valley) rather than in Jerusalem or a major city like Sepphoris. Many of Jesus's disciples were Galilean (John 1:40–49). Like Nathanael, they internalized the low expectations assigned to them and to a Galilean like Jesus. When Jesus performed his first miracle, it was a miracle designed to defeat these low expectations. It worked. When Jesus turned water into wine at a wedding in Cana of Galilee, "his disciples believed in him" (John 2:11).

INFORMATION 📍 along Highway 79; 🧭

MAPS

The Promised Land in the Time of the Bible

Old Testament and New Testament Cities

Sidon

Damascus

Litani R.

Mt. Hermon

Tyre

Dan

Caesarea
Philippi

Lake Hula

Hazor

Mediterranean Sea

Acco/Ptolemais

Chorazin

Bethsaida
Julias

Capernaum

Magdala/Taricheae

Sea
of
Galilee

Hippos

Khirbet Kana

Tiberias

Sepphoris

Gath Hepher

Nazareth

Yarmuk R.

Gadara

Kishon R.

Shunem

Megiddo

Jezreel

Caesarea Maritima

Beth Shan/Scythopolis

Pella

Ramoth Gilead

Dothan

Jabesh Gilead

Jordan R.

Sebaste Samaria

Tirzah

Gerasa (Jerash)

Mt. Ebal

Sychar

Mt. Gerizim

Shechem

Jabbok R.

Yarkon R.

Shiloh

Adam

Joppa

Gibeon

Bethel

Emmaus? (Qubeibeh)

Jericho (OT)

Amman (Rabbah/Philadelphia)

Gezer

Gibeah
of Saul

Jericho (NT)

Heshbon

Ekron

Aijalon

Kirlath
Jearim

Jerusalem

Mt. Nebo

Ashdod

Beth Shemesh

Bethany

Qumran

Medeba

Gath

Azekah

Bethlehem

Ashkelon

Herodium

Lachish

Dibon

Gaza

Hebron

Dead
Sea

En Gedi

Arnon R.

Gerar

Masada

Arad

Beersheba

Bozrah

Zoar?

Zered Brook

Tamar

235

Kadesh Barnea

Punon

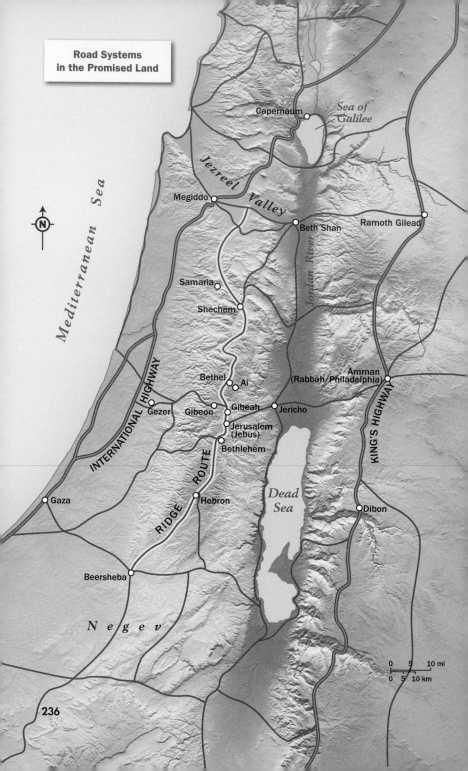

Road Systems in the Promised Land

Capernaum

Sea of Galilee

Jezreel Valley

Megiddo

Beth Shan

Ramoth Gilead

Mediterranean Sea

N

Samaria

Shechem

Jordan River

Bethel

Ai

Gibeah

Amman
(Rabbah / Philadelphia)

Gezer

Gibeon

Jericho

Jerusalem
(Jebus)

Bethlehem

INTERNATIONAL HIGHWAY

RIDGE ROUTE

KING'S HIGHWAY

Dead Sea

Gaza

Hebron

Dibon

Beersheba

N e g e v

0   5   10 mi
0   5   10 km

236

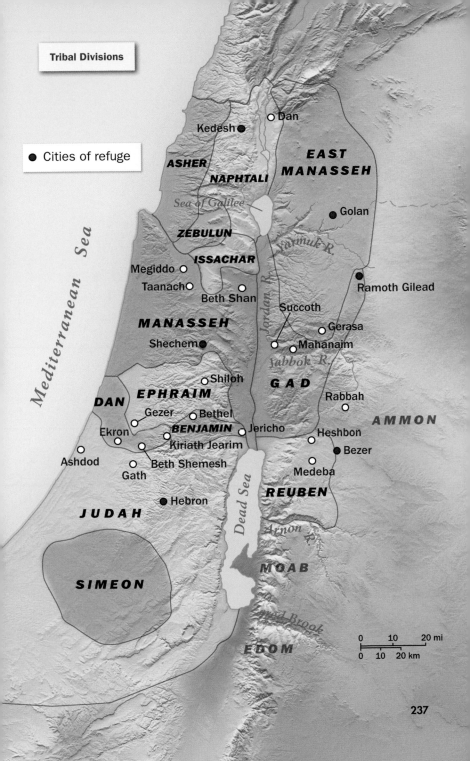

Tribal Divisions

● Cities of refuge

Mediterranean Sea

Dan
Kedesh ●

ASHER
NAPHTALI

EAST
MANASSEH

Sea of Galilee

Golan ●

ZEBULUN

ISSACHAR

Megiddo ○
Taanach ○
Beth Shan ○

Yarmuk R.

Ramoth Gilead ●

Succoth

Gerasa ○

MANASSEH

Shechem ●

Mahanaim
○

Jordan R.

Jabbok R.

Shiloh ○

GAD

DAN

EPHRAIM

Gezer ○ Bethel ○

BENJAMIN

Jericho ○

Rabbah ○

AMMON

Ekron ○

Kiriath Jearim ○

Heshbon ○

Ashdod ○

Beth Shemesh ○

Bezer ●

Gath ○

Medeba ○

REUBEN

Hebron ●

Dead Sea

JUDAH

Arnon R.

MOAB

SIMEON

Zered Brook

EDOM

| 0 | 10 | 20 mi |
| 0 | 10 | 20 km |

237

The United Kingdom

Mediterranean Sea

PHOENICIA

Tadmor

Sidon

Litani River

Damascus

Tyre

Dan

ARAM

Kadesh of Galilee

Sea of
Galilee

Acco

Hazor

Yarmuk River

Megiddo

Beth Shan

Ramoth Gilead

Shechem

Jabbok River

Gezer

Gibeon

GAD

AMMON

Joppa

Jericho

Ashdod

Rabbah

Beth Shemesh

Jerusalem

GILEAD

Gath

Dead Sea

Gaza

Hebron

Dibon

Aroer

Arad

Arnon River

Beersheba

MOAB

Zered Brook

NEGEV

EDOM

Kadesh Barnea

Petra

Ezion Geber

Gulf of Aqaba

Mt. Sinai?

Core territory of Israel ruled
by David and Solomon

Area strongly influenced by David
(after his wars) and Solomon

0   25   50 mi
0 25 50 km

Red Sea

The Divided Kingdom

Sidon

Damascus

Tyre

Dan

ARAM

PHOENICIA

Hazor

Mediterranean Sea

Acco

Sea of Galilee

Dor

Megiddo

Jezreel

Beth Shan

Ramoth Gilead

Taanach

Jordan River

ISRAEL

Samaria

Tirzah

Shechem

AMMON

Aphek

Joppa

Zorah

Bethel

Moresheth Gath

Gezer

Rabbah

Ekron

Mizpah

Heshbon

Ashdod

Gath

Ramah

Jerusalem

Ashkelon

Azekah

Bethlehem

Sokoh

Adullam

Gaza

Beth Zur

Lachish

Dibon

Adoraim

Hebron

Ziph

PHILISTIA

Dead Sea

JUDAH

Arad

MOAB

Beersheba

EDOM

Kadesh Barnea

Bozrah

0   10   20 mi
0 10 20 km

Israel in the Time of the New Testament

Mediterranean Sea

Sidon

SYRIA

Damascus

△ Mt. Hermon

Tyre

PHOENICIA

Caesarea Philippi

GAULANITIS

Trachonitis

Batanae

Acco/ Ptolemais

GALILEE

Capernaum

Bethsaida

Cana

Sepphoris

Tiberias

Hippos

Mt. Carmel △

Nazareth

Sea of Galilee

Auranitis

Caesarea Maritima

DECAPOLIS

Pella

SAMARIA

Sebaste

Gerasa (Jerash)

Antipatris

Sychar

Mt. Gerizim △

Joppa

PEREA

Philadelphia

Emmaus

Jericho

Jerusalem

Qumran

Bethlehem

Medeba

Ashkelon

Azotus

J U D E A

Machaerus

Hebron

Dead Sea

IDUMEA

Masada

Beersheba

NABATEA

Herod Antipas

Philip

Archelaus and successors

0   5   10 mi
0   5   10 km

240

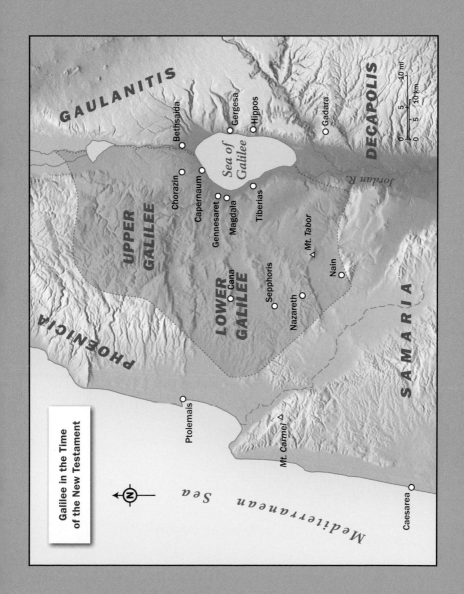

Galilee in the Time
of the New Testament

GAULANITIS

DECAPOLIS

Bethsaida

Gergesa

Hippos

Gadara

Sea of
Galilee

Jordan R.

UPPER
GALILEE

Chorazin

Capernaum

Gennesaret

Magdala

Tiberias

Mt. Tabor

LOWER
GALILEE

Cana

Sepphoris

Nain

Nazareth

SAMARIA

PHOENICIA

Ptolemais

Mt. Carmel

Caesarea

Mediterranean Sea

N

10 mi

5

10 km

5

0

0

BIBLE TIME LINE

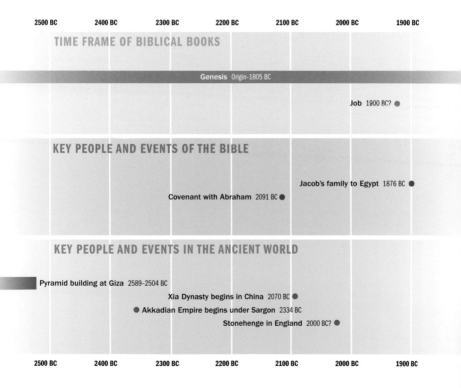

2500 BC	2400 BC	2300 BC	2200 BC	2100 BC	2000 BC	1900 BC

TIME FRAME OF BIBLICAL BOOKS

Genesis Origin–1805 BC

Job 1900 BC? ●

KEY PEOPLE AND EVENTS OF THE BIBLE

Jacob's family to Egypt 1876 BC ●

Covenant with Abraham 2091 BC ●

KEY PEOPLE AND EVENTS IN THE ANCIENT WORLD

Pyramid building at Giza 2589–2504 BC

Xia Dynasty begins in China 2070 BC ●

● Akkadian Empire begins under Sargon 2334 BC

Stonehenge in England 2000 BC? ●

2500 BC	2400 BC	2300 BC	2200 BC	2100 BC	2000 BC	1900 BC

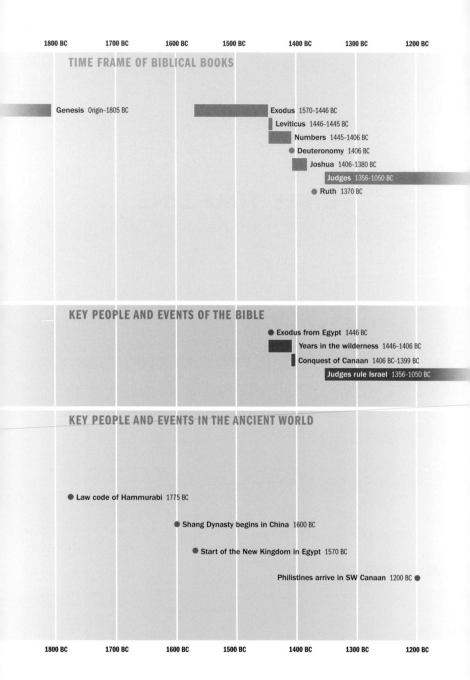

| | 1800 BC | 1700 BC | 1600 BC | 1500 BC | 1400 BC | 1300 BC | 1200 BC |

TIME FRAME OF BIBLICAL BOOKS

Genesis Origin–1805 BC

Exodus 1570–1446 BC

Leviticus 1446–1445 BC

Numbers 1445–1406 BC

Deuteronomy 1406 BC

Joshua 1406–1380 BC

Judges 1356–1050 BC

Ruth 1370 BC

KEY PEOPLE AND EVENTS OF THE BIBLE

Exodus from Egypt 1446 BC

Years in the wilderness 1446–1406 BC

Conquest of Canaan 1406 BC–1399 BC

Judges rule Israel 1356–1050 BC

KEY PEOPLE AND EVENTS IN THE ANCIENT WORLD

Law code of Hammurabi 1775 BC

Shang Dynasty begins in China 1600 BC

Start of the New Kingdom in Egypt 1570 BC

Philistines arrive in SW Canaan 1200 BC

| | 1800 BC | 1700 BC | 1600 BC | 1500 BC | 1400 BC | 1300 BC | 1200 BC |

244

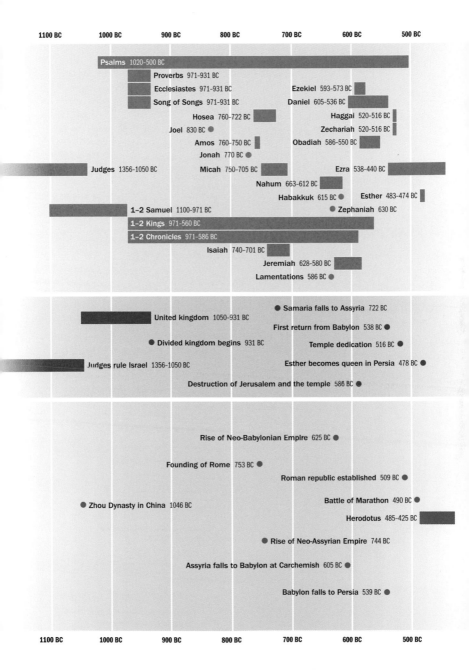

1100 BC   1000 BC   900 BC   800 BC   700 BC   600 BC   500 BC

Psalms 1020–500 BC

Proverbs 971–931 BC
Ecclesiastes 971–931 BC
Song of Songs 971–931 BC
Hosea 760–722 BC
Joel 830 BC
Amos 760–750 BC
Jonah 770 BC
Judges 1356–1050 BC
Micah 750–705 BC
Nahum 663–612 BC
Habakkuk 615 BC
1–2 Samuel 1100–971 BC
1–2 Kings 971–560 BC
1–2 Chronicles 971–586 BC
Isaiah 740–701 BC
Jeremiah 628–580 BC
Lamentations 586 BC

Ezekiel 593–573 BC
Daniel 605–536 BC
Haggai 520–516 BC
Zechariah 520–516 BC
Obadiah 586–550 BC
Ezra 538–440 BC
Esther 483–474 BC
Zephaniah 630 BC

Samaria falls to Assyria 722 BC
United kingdom 1050–931 BC
First return from Babylon 538 BC
Divided kingdom begins 931 BC
Temple dedication 516 BC
Judges rule Israel 1356–1050 BC
Esther becomes queen in Persia 478 BC
Destruction of Jerusalem and the temple 586 BC

Rise of Neo-Babylonian Empire 625 BC
Founding of Rome 753 BC
Roman republic established 509 BC
Zhou Dynasty in China 1046 BC
Battle of Marathon 490 BC
Herodotus 485–425 BC
Rise of Neo-Assyrian Empire 744 BC
Assyria falls to Babylon at Carchemish 605 BC
Babylon falls to Persia 539 BC

1100 BC   1000 BC   900 BC   800 BC   700 BC   600 BC   500 BC

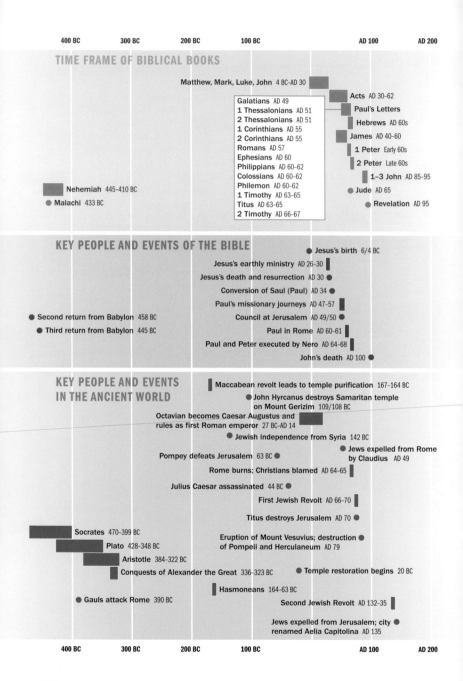

TIME FRAME OF BIBLICAL BOOKS

Matthew, Mark, Luke, John 4 BC–AD 30

Galatians AD 49
1 Thessalonians AD 51
2 Thessalonians AD 51
1 Corinthians AD 55
2 Corinthians AD 55
Romans AD 57
Ephesians AD 60
Philippians AD 60–62
Colossians AD 60–62
Philemon AD 60–62
1 Timothy AD 63–65
Titus AD 63–65
2 Timothy AD 66–67

Acts AD 30–62
Paul's Letters
Hebrews AD 60s
James AD 40–60
1 Peter Early 60s
2 Peter Late 60s
1–3 John AD 85–95
Jude AD 65
Revelation AD 95

Nehemiah 445–410 BC
Malachi 433 BC

KEY PEOPLE AND EVENTS OF THE BIBLE

Jesus's birth 6/4 BC
Jesus's earthly ministry AD 26–30
Jesus's death and resurrection AD 30
Conversion of Saul (Paul) AD 34
Paul's missionary journeys AD 47–57
Second return from Babylon 458 BC
Council at Jerusalem AD 49/50
Third return from Babylon 445 BC
Paul in Rome AD 60–61
Paul and Peter executed by Nero AD 64–68
John's death AD 100

KEY PEOPLE AND EVENTS
IN THE ANCIENT WORLD

Maccabean revolt leads to temple purification 167–164 BC
John Hyrcanus destroys Samaritan temple
on Mount Gerizim 109/108 BC
Octavian becomes Caesar Augustus and
rules as first Roman emperor 27 BC–AD 14
Jewish independence from Syria 142 BC
Jews expelled from Rome
by Claudius AD 49
Pompey defeats Jerusalem 63 BC
Rome burns; Christians blamed AD 64–65
Julius Caesar assassinated 44 BC
First Jewish Revolt AD 66–70
Titus destroys Jerusalem AD 70
Socrates 470–399 BC
Eruption of Mount Vesuvius; destruction
Plato 428–348 BC
of Pompeii and Herculaneum AD 79
Aristotle 384–322 BC
Conquests of Alexander the Great 336–323 BC
Temple restoration begins 20 BC
Hasmoneans 164–63 BC
Gauls attack Rome 390 BC
Second Jewish Revolt AD 132–35
Jews expelled from Jerusalem; city
renamed Aelia Capitolina AD 135

INDEX of LOCATIONS

Note: References in ***red italics*** are to visual material (maps, charts, and illustrations).

Resources that
Bring the Bible to Life

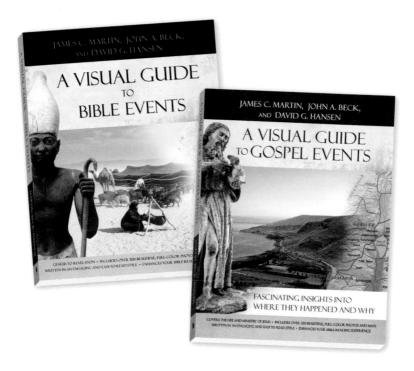

These beautiful, full-color books include hundreds of photographs and maps that bring the ancient world to life. The engaging writing style makes these resources perfect for anyone—student, scholar, pastor, or layperson—who wants to understand biblical and Gospel events in a deeper way.

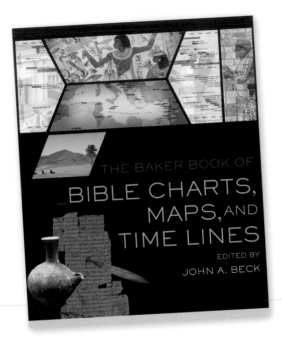